THOMAS AND LYSANDRA
OSTERKAMP

Happily NEVER After

5 WAYS TO DESTROY OR CREATE YOUR FAIRY TALE

ALSO BY LYSANDRA OSTERKAMP

Balancing the Crazy

THOMAS AND LYSANDRA
OSTERKAMP

Happily NEVER After

5 WAYS TO DESTROY OR CREATE YOUR FAIRY TALE

Contents

Introduction

Where's My Fairy Tale?

Once upon a time . . . there was a girl whose dreams were coming true.

She was overjoyed as her wedding day drew ever closer and her happily ever after would begin. Everything was going to be flawless—the whole day—the white dress, the flowers, the tuxedos, the handsome groom, and the future. She just knew she was getting everything she ever wanted—the man who loved her, the happy marriage, the sweet little babies that would be born, and the cute little house. It was all happening as she imagined years ago. Everything was going to be lovely. It would be perfect.

Three short months later, only weeks after the wedding, this hopeful new bride's dreams were smashed by the sad reality of what marriage truly is. This disappointed young wife sat crying on the bathroom floor as her exhausted, confused husband sat on the bed outside the door in utter disenchantment. Both wondered separately, "Where's my happily ever after?"

Why is it that what we dream rarely becomes a reality? Why does marriage often feel like happily *never* after?

Lysandra

I'm the disappointed young wife. Not because my Thomas was a bad husband; he was quite adequate at the time. I felt great disappointment because marriage wasn't what I dreamed it would be. I wasn't living the fairy tale I had looked forward to my whole life. I was newly married; there was fighting, misunderstandings, and resentment. I was living happily never after.

Thomas

I'm the confused husband. Lysandra was the girl of my dreams, but why wasn't she just happy? I thought everything was fine in our life. Then, finally, I realized there was a problem. My first clue was that my brand-new bride cried; she cried a lot. I didn't think it would be like this. I thought we'd get married, and I'd make her happy. I thought it would be relatively easy to make someone you love so deeply, happy. I was wrong. No one in this apartment was happy.

Isn't marriage supposed to make you happy? Aren't you supposed to get married, then ride off into the sunset and enjoy happiness till death do us part?

The answer is *no*. I think we all know that isn't reality, yet we can't help ourselves from dreaming that what we have will be the exception to the rule. We will be the ones to get the fairy tale.

We will enjoy a mythical happily ever after.

Our Love Story

The beginning of a relationship is so fun! A person catches your eye, you're attracted to them, they seem so perfect, and then that amazing feeling when they reciprocate interest. Your eyes are wide open. It's new, it's exciting, it's romantic. The butterflies are dancing around in your stomach every time you think about them, every time you're on your way to see them, and every time you're near each other. Then the dreaming begins. Is this the *one*? What would forever look like with them? Is this the beginning of happily ever after for me?

In the beginning our story was exciting, new, and romantic, complete with butterflies in the stomach. We met in church when we were in elementary school. Neither of us liked each other when we were children. It wasn't until middle school that we would notice one another in that lovey-dovey way. We say it's all thanks to Wanda Rutan, a beautiful, sweet, prayer warrior and matchmaker in our church. She hired both of us to make fishing lures for her husband's business to raise money for Bible camp. Mrs. Rutan always made sure we were working the same days; she made sure we worked together and sat by each other. She was shamelessly setting us up and we're so glad she did! We often thank God for our sweet Wanda.

Thomas

I remember the exact moment I fell in love with Lysandra. My family was grocery shopping when I walked around the corner of an aisle and saw the Gilchrist family. They had just come from the airport returning from a family vacation in Orlando, Florida.

They had stopped at the store for groceries before heading home.

There was something unusual about Lysandra this time which made me notice her in a new and different way. It wasn't some unknown, mysterious, emotional element. It was obvious. It was visual. She was a blonde, fair-skinned Iowa girl who had spent a solid week in the Florida sun in the middle of February. She was completely sunburnt. Her face was as bright red as a strawberry. I couldn't help but notice her!

I stared at her. She kept moving so my view of her would be blocked by her dad, but every step she took, I took one too. I couldn't get enough of her. I fell in love that night. I couldn't get her out of my head from that day on.

That was the night I began my lifelong pursuit of Lysandra. I rode my bicycle three miles to church early every Sunday and Wednesday to get a little extra time to be in her presence. Every time Mrs. Rutan said she was working I made sure I was there too. I knew Mrs. Rutan would do the rest. If there was an opportunity to be near Lysandra, I took it. After a couple of months of flirting, I worked up the nerve to tell her how I felt.

It was just seven short years later when I convinced her to marry me! It was an unusually warm Midwest January day when I took her to the flower garden across from the Cedar River where we used to walk when we'd spend time together. I had my brother, Chris, strategically hiding in the bushes with a video camera. I sat Lysandra down on a cement bench and got down on one knee. I held out the ring I chose for her and asked her to be my wife.

Lysandra was so excited she shouted "Yes!" and flung her arms in the air to hug me. When she did, she knocked the ring out of my hand and into a pile of dead leaves. I frantically searched for the ring as she hugged my neck.

We had a fantastic time planning the wedding together. We talked and dreamed of our new life together. Then my dreams came true on August 2, 2003. Lysandra was the most beautiful bride in the world as she walked down the aisle toward me. I still love the picture our photographer took of me while I watched Lysandra walk toward me: you can see the sheer joy on my face. It was the moment I had dreamed of for seven years.

We thought this was the beginning of our happily ever after, but it was happily never after instead.

Lysandra

All my dreams were coming true that day too. As early as I can remember, I wanted to get married and have a happy little family. It turns out my dreams were unrealistic, and the dream world crumbled pretty quickly. I was the heroine of my imaginary fairy tale. Basically, when I envisioned marriage, I was very selfish. It was all about me—my adventure, my dreams coming true, my prince charming fawning over me all the time and doing everything for the sole purpose of making me happy. I thought marriage was going to be about me.

Thomas

I never dreamed of a fairy tale. Or, at least, I didn't think of it that way. I just dreamed of having Lysandra near me all the time. I wanted her to be available to me all the time without end. I wanted to get married to be together forever. I wanted to be happy. That was my fairy tale, I guess.

Not What We Imagined

Marriage wasn't what either of us thought it would be. Marriage was difficult, and sometimes it felt impossible. We fought, we cried, we hurt each other, we messed up, and we lost our tempers. It was a hot mess, especially at the beginning.

We always laugh when people tell us we're lucky because we've always had a perfect marriage. The relationship we've had has been far from perfect, and there was no luck involved at all. We worked intentionally to invest in our relationship with each other, but most importantly, we made the majority of our lives, separately and together, a pursuit of God. It's only by the grace of God that we stuck it out and made it this far.

This isn't a perfectly enchanted love story. This is a grim story of two imperfect people becoming one.

Five chapters of this book highlight five ways to destroy your fairy tale. In these chapters we become transparent and openly share with you our stories of what we did to destroy happiness in our marriage.

The other five chapters describe five ways to create your fairy tale. In these chapters we share what we've learned after twenty years of marriage. We want to share with you the things we wish we knew twenty years ago so that you can enjoy your marriage relationship the way we do now.

Being married can be amazing! We are best friends and love being together. We have more fun together than we ever imagined possible. Doing this life with each other is not just good but great! We want you to know, you can have what we have. God can do in your marriage what He has done in ours and replace your happily *never* after with His happily *ever* after.

1

Define Fairy Tale

My Happiness = My Fairy Tale

Once upon a time . . . there was boy who fell in love with a girl.

Unfortunately for him, she didn't love him back. He pursued her and did everything in his power to win her heart. One day, he worked up the nerve to confess his love for her. He whispered to her so no one else could hear, "Meet me outside."

He waited outside, his hands sweating, his legs a little weak. To his surprise and delight, she walked around the corner! He gathered all the courage that he could muster, put his heart on the line, and said it. "I love you." His heart was beating so hard that it felt like it would pop right out of his chest. He waited what felt like forever for those four words in return—I love you too.

Those words never came. He said I love you to her every time that he saw her for the next seven years. For seven years she would say what no one ever wants to hear after saying I love you. She would say, "I care about you too."

Thomas

Not exactly the fairy tale I had in mind. My fairy tale went something like this . . .

Once upon a time, there was a boy who fell in love with a girl. She loved him back with all her heart. They got married, had lots of sex, and lived happily ever after.

I thought it was uncomplicated, but the simple fairy tales that we write for ourselves rarely become reality. The fairy tale that I wrote for myself was straightforward. I love the girl. She loves me back. I'm happy forever. Simple, right? Apparently not.

Lysandra

It wasn't my fairy tale either. I wanted the knight in shining armor who was basically perfect or at least my definition of perfect. I liked Thomas and everything, but he had some glaringly obvious imperfections. I knew that I didn't love him, and I refused to lie to him. I told him the truth, "I care about you."

I wanted more than what he was offering me. I wanted a guy who was just as excited about Jesus as I was. I was selfish. I wanted to get to choose where we went and how we lived. I wanted to do something great for God, yet even in that, it was about me being happy because it's what I wanted. I wanted someone who would essentially live to make me happy. My happiness was at the heart of my fairy tale.

The Illusion

There is a widely accepted myth in our culture that to live happily ever after we must chase happiness. We are told that we are responsible for our own happiness. Only you can advocate for yourself. Self-care is the priority. Make choices for yourself. You do you. Live for yourself. Do as you please. If you want it, take it. Your story is about you. Your life is about your happiness.

We've taken this illusion so far as to believe that everything in our lives is about what makes us happy. It makes logical sense that this philosophy and way of living would transfer over into our marriages. We have convinced ourselves that our marriages are about pleasing ourselves.

Believing this myth is a surefire way to destroy your fairy tale.

This is contradictory to what we see in Scripture. We aren't supposed to live for ourselves or our own happiness. Look at what Paul wrote in *2 Corinthians 5:15, "he died for all, that those who live might no longer live for themselves but for him who for their sake died and was raised."*

Focusing on your pleasure will not bring you joy, but sorrow. Seeking to please yourself will be empty. Chasing your happiness will create a beast inside of you that will take over your life, snuffing out every hope of a true happily ever after.

This isn't what the princess cartoons tell us. They show us a damsel in distress who is rescued by a handsome prince from a dragon, exile, an evil sea monster, or chores (which are just as bad as the first three). The two of them get married and live a life of ease where they get to do whatever they want, and their own happiness is the key to their fairy tale.

We subconsciously take this model into our marriages. The problem is that this model of chasing our own happiness is an absolute disaster when implemented off the screen and in reality. Susanna Newsonen notes in an article in *Psychology Today*:

> *The chase [for happiness] is making people anxious. It's making people overwhelmed. It's making people feel pressure that they have to be happy, all the time. This is a big problem, but luckily, it's a solvable one. A lot of the anxiety and pressure around happiness come from societal*

misunderstandings about what happiness is. These misunderstandings drive us to unknowingly chase happiness out of our lives . . .[1]

Lysandra

I did fall in love with Thomas, eventually. Seven years after he first confessed his love for me, I said, "I love you too." It was really nice to be in love, get engaged, plan a wedding, and prepare for a marriage. It appeared my fairy tale, while different than I envisioned, was playing out before my eyes. I was in the middle of my own rom-com! I was happy—for a while.

The fairy tale I was trying to create portrayed me as the heroine princess. I was the center of the story. We got married and moved a significantly long distance away from home. We now lived in a little apartment in Pensacola, Florida, where Thomas was the only person that I knew.

I became sad. I cried a lot. I had big emotional mood swings. I missed my family, was lonely, and I felt like Thomas wasn't meeting all my needs. This story wasn't what I had written. I wrote a fairy tale where I was happy all the time because my husband doted over me and gave in to my every whim. If anyone knows Thomas, he's not the type to give in easily, especially not when he was twenty-two!

I was miserable. I had chased my happiness right into a dungeon of despair. Doesn't marriage sound great?

Thomas

My fairy tale wasn't turning out so great either. I know Lysandra felt like I was getting my way all the time, but that's not what I remember. I was constantly trying to make her happy, and she was constantly crying!

This season of our marriage did a great job of preparing

me for our four daughters, especially when they were younger. They would cry, and I would do my best Sherlock Holmes impression and try to figure out what was wrong. I figured out that I am not even on Dr. Watson's level, never mind Sherlock Holmes. I would offer them toys, food, and candy, but it seemed like nothing worked. Which isn't surprising because I could never figure it out with Lysandra either.

I thought once I got married, I was going to have sex whenever I wanted, but she would get mad and not want to even touch me. My happily ever after turned out to be happily never after. I wasn't happy much of the time, but I wasn't giving up on happiness.

I found things that made me happy like playing video games with my college buddies. I would have the guys over after classes. We would hang out and play *WWE Smackdown* on my PlayStation into the night. We had such a great time together. It was all-night fun, but the fun stopped when Lysandra came home from work.

She opened the door, saw us having a great time, and got mad instantly. She was like Robocop, but instead of wasting criminals, she was dead set on killing all my fun. It didn't make any sense to me. Wasn't a wife supposed to want her husband to be happy? Wasn't her job to ensure my happiness? She sure was doing a terrible job of it.

Lysandra

What about me? Wasn't it the husband's job to make his wife happy? Especially when he dragged her hours and hours away from her family to a place where she didn't know anyone? Wouldn't he want to do everything in his power to make her feel loved, appreciated, and happy?

Yes, I was mad when I got home. I had worked eight hours at IHOP serving pancakes, working hard for every tip to pay his school bill. I then changed my apron and worked another six hours waiting tables at Village Inn to pay our bills. I was so worn out and empty that I could barely stay awake on the drive home. I imagine that this is exactly what Cinderella felt like.

I was sure that my new husband had gone to classes, studied, cleaned the house, and prepared supper for me in gratitude for my hours of labor that day. Only to walk into our little apartment and find his friends living their best life sprawled out in our living room, dirty dishes on the coffee table and all over the kitchen, trash everywhere, everyone laughing and yelling at the TV.

All I wanted was to eat something, have my sore feet rubbed, and go to bed. It looked like that wasn't going to happen. I was furious! I was a long, long way from happy. Happiness looked like a dot in the distance of my rearview mirror. My fairy tale was turning out to be a horror story. The worst part of it all was that Thomas made *me* out to be the villain! Where's my happily ever after?

The Storybook Deception

When you buy into the myth that your marriage is about making you happy, you are deceived. All those fairy tales we read about in colorful storybooks, all those princess movies we watched and sang along to our entire childhood, and all those romantic comedies we were convinced would one day happen to us set us up to fall into the "me-centered happiness deception."

We are human beings. We are not characters in a romantic storybook. We were created and designed by a loving, thoughtful Creator. His design for us was not to be obsessed with what we believe will make us happy. In fact, He fully knows where that path leads—to death and destruction. He designed us for more. He designed us to follow His plan, and that master plan would ensure inner peace and a fullness of joy that cannot be compared to any momentary happiness we can achieve. Remember what Jesus told the crowds in Luke 9:23–25:

> *And he said to all, 'If anyone would come after me, let him deny himself and take up his cross daily and follow me. For whoever would save his life will lose it, but whoever loses his life for my sake will save it. For what does it profit a man if he gains the whole world and loses or forfeits himself?'*

The me-centered happiness deception says that everything and everyone in my life should make me happy, including my spouse and my marriage. God tells us in Galatians 5:24, *"those who belong to Christ Jesus have crucified the flesh with its passions and desires."*

When two pleasure seekers live their lives believing the happiness deception (where everyone and everything in their lives is about their happiness), get married, and continue to live this way, they are going in opposite directions. Each are the center of their own world.

The husband is on a trajected course to pursue his own happiness, while the wife is on her separate journey searching for everything that makes her happy. They are traveling in opposite directions and will continue to travel further away from each other and further away from true happiness.

GOD

Time goes on and the marriage gets cold and stale. The distance between them is staggering, although it happened slowly over the years. There's a chill in the house, and the bedroom is as frozen as Elsa's ice castle.

The wife is pursuing her career and her goals. She finds fleeting moments of happiness when she gets a promotion, or she sees success in her children. She may have a little joy when she's out with her friends. She chases those moments of happiness by throwing all that she has into her work, her children, and her friends. Resentment creeps in at the thought that her husband isn't living his life to make her happy. She feels unloved, undervalued, unsatisfied, and unhappy.

The husband's path is similar to the wife's, but it's in the opposite direction. He feels fulfillment in being a good provider. When he can afford to take the family on vacation or buy that newer SUV, he has a brief feeling of happiness. It doesn't last very long because there's always more money to be made and more things to buy. He runs down the path of success looking for that next hit of joy. He is angry that his wife doesn't care enough about him to live her life to make him happy. He sees her as selfish and cold. He feels disrespected and dissatisfied, and he becomes disengaged.

This isn't a happy marriage. This is a couple of roommates who resent one another. And maybe this is exactly where you are in your marriage. It doesn't have to be this way.

When a husband and a wife are pursuing their own happiness in life and marriage, they are most definitely traveling in opposite directions. No two people become happy with the exact same thing. I'm in it for me, and you're in it for you. Opposite directions. Separated. Happily *never* after.

The Paradox

Chasing your own happiness brings sorrow. When you

pursue pleasure, you uncover despair. The longer you chase your happy the further you get from it.

Look at these words of warning Jesus gave us in Matthew 6:25–33. He unearths the truth about chasing your own happiness. It's amazing that even two thousand years ago the human race was chasing their own happiness and in doing so creating anxiety and fear, just as we are today.

> *"Therefore I tell you, do not be anxious about your life, what you will eat or what you will drink, nor about your body, what you will put on. Is not life more than food, and the body more than clothing? Look at the birds of the air: they neither sow nor reap nor gather into barns, and yet your heavenly Father feeds them. Are you not of more value than they? And which of you by being anxious can add a single hour to his span of life? And why are you anxious about clothing? Consider the lilies of the field, how they grow: they neither toil nor spin, yet I tell you, even Solomon in all his glory was not arrayed like one of these. But if God so clothes the grass of the field, which today is alive and tomorrow is thrown into the oven, will he not much more clothe you, O you of little faith? Therefore do not be anxious, saying, 'What shall we eat?' or 'What shall we drink?' or 'What shall we wear?' For the Gentiles seek after all these things, and your heavenly Father knows that you need them all. But seek first the kingdom of God and his righteousness, and all these things will be added to you. Therefore do not be anxious about tomorrow, for tomorrow will be anxious for itself. Sufficient for the day is its own trouble."*

Our world is so full of anxiety. This passage explains how we cause ourselves to be overcome with anxiety. When we focus on all the stuff, the relationships, and the love that we think we need to make us happy, we actually create a life of anxiety for ourselves. Striving for happiness is exhausting! It will tear you down. It will rewrite your fairy tale into a horror story.

This is the paradox. It doesn't make sense. If I work toward pleasing myself, if I set everything up in my life to achieve happiness, if my spouse would just put me first, I will be happy, right? Wrong.

That's why it is a paradox. If you work toward pleasing yourself, if you set everything up in your life to achieve happiness, if your spouse puts you first, you will not be happy. You will be full of sorrow and anxiety. You work so hard for it, exert all this energy towards it, hurt your relationship, and in the end, you don't get what you want anyway! You will destroy your fairy tale.

Thomas

I believed that my happiness was found in doing what I wanted to do. I thought if I got my way, I would be happy. Nothing showed me how wrong I was like our first trip back to Iowa after being married for just four short months.

Lysandra was so excited to go home and see her family. To say that we didn't have very much money at the time is an extreme understatement, but we had enough money to put gas in the tank and drive from Pensacola, Florida, to Cedar Rapids, Iowa. My brother was in college during this time and stayed at our house most weekends. He was riding back to Iowa with us. We drove for twelve hours into the night. That's when we heard some unusual sounds coming from the engine. The car eventually rolled to a stop on the side of the interstate.

It was December in Missouri, and it was freezing outside! We had cell phones at this time, but no Internet to look up any phone numbers. So, we called Lysandra's parents who called a tow truck for us. The only thing that we could do was sit on the side of the road and wait.

I could see Lysandra was devastated and fighting back tears. She just wanted to be home with her family for Christmas. But to be honest, it didn't bother me at all that the car had broken down. I was with my brother, I wasn't doing schoolwork, and I got to stay in a hotel with cable! I felt like I was on vacation. This was my dream, but this was Lysandra's nightmare!

The mechanic checked out the car, and it was really bad news. We were stuck in Sikeston, Missouri, for three days and two nights. My brother and I had a great time in the motel room eating chips, goofing off, and watching a marathon of *Most Extreme Elimination Challenge*. If you aren't sure what that is, it must be the stupidest yet most entertaining game show of all time. Lysandra didn't find it as funny as we did. She was miserable, but I didn't really care because I was happy, and in the beginning my happiness was the point.

Her misery and my selfishness created a dynamic that would become the norm in our marriage for many years. Nagging became a mainstay in our home. She would nag to try to get me to think of her happiness. I ignored what she wanted to get my own happiness. She nagged louder and more often, but the louder she nagged, the harder I fought for my happiness. She was angry and sad, and I was just angry. No one was happy. Marriage was miserable. This same story is repeated in marriages all over the world.

Lysandra

To this day, I can't drive past Sikeston, Missouri, without getting a sick feeling in my stomach. Those were some of the worst days of my life. We had no money. We were stuck in a tiny, dirty hotel room with my husband's brother while they laughed and watched TV shows that I hated. Seriously, what's so funny about a guy running full speed into a wall to try to win some lame prize? We didn't have enough money for real food, so I remember all that we could afford was a bag of apples and a bag of chips. I was bored, disappointed, and hangry.

I begged Thomas to go on walks with me, turn off the TV and talk to me, or do anything besides this. His answer was always the same—*no*. All that he cared about was his own happiness which made me angry. I didn't understand that I was only angry because all that I cared about was my own happiness. The truth is our marriage was miserable because we were both pursuing our own version of happy.

Neither of us had any thought about pleasing God or pleasing one another during that dreadful stay in Sikeston, Missouri. Eventually, my parents drove the six hours from Iowa to pick us up and take us home for Christmas, but even during that Christmas holiday both Thomas and I had resentment for one another. There were moments of happiness, but not true joy in our marriage.

Chasing Happiness Destroys Happiness

When you are driven by your own pleasures and desires you are opening yourself up to dissatisfaction, discontentment, strife, and ultimately broken relationships. What drives you? What's your goal in life? What's your goal in marriage? Have you ever given it any thought? Take a minute to think about what you want out of your marriage. When you identify your goal for your marriage you uncover what you're pursuing.

Marriage was not designed to make you happy. We love what Tony Evans writes at the beginning of his book *Kingdom Marriage*:

> *The problem today is that we have transposed the benefit of marriage with the goal, so that when the benefit-happiness-is not working out, we quit and move on, or we*

resign ourselves to living a life of unhappiness." "Marriage is not merely a social contract; it is a sacred covenant. It is not simply a means of looking for love, happiness, and fulfillment. Those things are important; in fact, they are critical. Yet because we have put second things first, as important as second things are, we are having trouble living out either. When God's purpose and principles for marriage are undermined, His image becomes distorted, and our ability to influence others on God's behalf erodes. [2]

You were not created to operate in this way of chasing happiness. Happiness can be a benefit of marriage, but it should never become the goal. God didn't intend you to pursue your own pleasure in your marriage. Any time a created being is operating outside of the Creator's design it malfunctions and cannot operate to its fullest potential. While chasing your own happiness, you will destroy your fairy tale.

2

Redefine Fairy Tale

Making God's Plan Our Purpose

Once upon a time . . . there were a husband and wife who rewrote their definition of fairy tale.

Thomas

It's funny to think back to twenty years ago when we first got married and remember my vision of my perfect life and marriage. I really thought we would live happily ever after. Happiness in marriage was so simple in my mind and so utterly complicated in reality.

I can't remember when it happened. I wish I could say it was after a knockdown drag out fight when we both submitted to God's plan rather than our own happiness. I wish I could tell you some heartwarming story about the two of us realizing the error of our ways after a dramatic sermon, crying in repentance together for our self-centeredness, and changing our focus.

That's not how it happened. It happened slowly. It happened as years passed, hard times came, and life beat us up a bit. It's almost like we had to try our own hand at happiness and fail before we could fully understand that achieving our own happiness couldn't be grasped. It's just like Jesus's story of the prodigal son. That son went out and tried everything to find his own happiness. Once he had tried everything and wasted all that he had, he realized the error of his self-seeking behavior.

Somewhere around year seven, we stopped focusing on our own happiness and started pursuing God. Don't get me wrong, we always kept God in our marriage. We were both followers of Jesus before we got married. I was a pastor from the beginning of our marriage. We were always in church, serving Jesus, serving others, reading the Bible, and praying. You know, checking all the Christian boxes.

The focus for years, when it came to my marriage was, how can Lysandra make me happy? How can I be happy in this marriage? How can I feel satisfied and fulfilled? How can I live my fairy tale? We were okay, but there was an emptiness felt. We looked fine on the outside, but we were each selfish and self-seeking. There was an underlying animosity and resentment. There was friction between us as we both pursued our own happiness in our own way.

That all changed when we redefined our fairy tale.

Lysandra

I'm thirty-eight now and have been married for twenty years. It took time, but my definition of fairy tale has changed. No longer am I chasing the imaginary storybook love that supposedly brings unending happiness. I tried that. I understand that it doesn't exist; it isn't real.

Seeking picture-perfect scenarios is a thing of the past. Through difficulty I learned to let go of the video montage I used to see in my mind of horseback riding on the beach at sunset, wind blowing in our hair, my beautiful dress flowing behind me without a care in the world. I want more.

Now I want heart satisfaction, inner peace, and consistent joy. I want the impossible. Thomas can't offer me these things, nor can I gain them myself. There's only one way to enjoy a life of heart satisfaction, inner peace, and consistent joy. It is only through Jesus. Not in just knowing Him, but in seeking Him above all else, setting Him up as first place in my life, making my purpose in life to please Him.

I can speak from experience; this is the real fairy-tale life. It's pursuing God with my whole heart and watching Him take care of the rest. When I pursue Him above my own idea of happiness, the "rest" is better than I ever dreamed it could be! I'm living out the Apostle Paul's words in in my marriage: "*Now to him who is able to do far more abundantly than all that we ask or think, according to the power at work within us, to him be glory*" (Ephesians 3:20–21).

What's a Fairy Tale Anyway?

Our culture tells you a fairy-tale romance involves a tall, dark, handsome, muscular guy falling head over heels for a gorgeous, slender, perfect girl. She falls madly in love with him. He proposes; she says *yes*. She wears the perfect white gown and walks down the aisle while he looks at her in utter amazement. The two get married. They are happy. They never fight or have any kind of conflict. A perfect life is implied. They ride off into the sunset and live happily ever after.

Merriam-Webster defines fairy tale as "a story in which improbable events lead to a happy ending." This tends to be our definition of fairy tale too. We want improbable perfection to happen to us. We want the rom-com where we're the star. We want that unlikely romance to lead to our happily ever after.

Every person believes they are the main character in their story and happiness is the goal. When we grow up watching the cartoon fairy tales and reading the fairy-tale children's books, a definition of happily ever after is created in our minds. Even as children the dreaming begins, and the definition is formed.

Let's Redefine Fairy Tale

What if there's more to marriage than this sequence of perfect, improbable events? What if life could be better than the best romantic comedy we've ever seen? What if marriage can be more fulfilling than the best story we've ever read in books?

It can be! But it only happens when we redefine what a fairy tale is. It happens when we allow God to write the story. True joy and inner peace happen when we submit to His authorship. Only He can create the best, most beautiful life for us.

It just makes sense to let the God who designed and created us be the One who tells us how to have a good, fulfilling, happy life. It's reasonable to allow the perfect Creator to give us our definition of happily ever after.

Let's look at God's definition of a fairy tale and a happy life and marriage, and what He promises for those that put Him first.

He promises abundant life in John 10:10b: "*I came that they may have life and have it abundantly.*"

He promises joy and peace in Romans 15:13: "*May the God of hope fill you with all joy and peace in believing, so that by the power of the Holy Spirit you may abound in hope.*"

He says that we will be blessed in Psalm 34:8: "*Oh, taste and see that the Lord is good! Blessed is the man who takes refuge in Him!*"

He promises happiness in Proverbs 16:20: "*Whoever gives thought to the word will discover good, and blessed is he who trusts in the Lord.*" And in Psalm 144:15: "*Blessed are the people whose God is the LORD!*"

He promises joy and pleasure in Psalm 16:11: "*You make known to me the path of life; in your presence there is fullness of joy; at your right hand are pleasures forevermore.*"

He promises to meet all our needs in Matthew 6:33: "*But seek first the kingdom of God and his righteousness, and all these things will be added to you.*"

We don't have to look out for ourselves. When we choose a life and a marriage that puts God first, He will look out for us. And He can do a far better job of it than we possibly can!

Lysandra

At some point in our marriage, I stopped being obsessed with getting my own way. At some point I realized my happiness was not what I wanted to chase anymore. I just wanted to chase Jesus.

I know there was a turning point for me when Thomas and I were counselling our first married couple with real problems. This was a couple comprised of two people who made happiness their goal and aim. They sought their own happiness from wherever and with whomever they thought they could find it.

Both the husband and the wife had participated in multiple extra-marital affairs. They had children as a result of the affairs. There were deep wounds and fierce anger. There were yelling, fighting, and crying in our office as we allowed them to share their story with us.

Then they turned to us and said, "Can you help us?" We instinctively said, "Yes, with the power of God, nothing is impossible. God can save your marriage."

I don't think either Thomas or I knew what we were going to say or what we would do to help them rebuild this relationship that had been battered, torn down, and burned to ashes.

But we knew that God was able to take anything that is ruined and make something beautiful out of it. Look what it says about Him in Isaiah 61:3: "*. . . to give them a beautiful headdress instead of ashes, the oil of gladness instead of mourning, the garment of praise instead of a faint spirit; that they may be called oaks of righteousness, the planting of the LORD, that he may be glorified.*"

I knew the Bible and I knew we serve the God of the impossible. I knew He could give them beauty for the ashes that was their marriage. So, we trusted God, we prayed, and we met once a week. God did a beautiful thing in their lives that I can't fully understand even today. He saved their marriage, which seemed beyond saving.

When they left that first day, Thomas shut the office door, he turned to me, and we hugged. We held each other for a while. We talked about how we didn't want that to be us. We talked about how we needed to prevent that from ever happening in our marriage. I think that was when we got serious about really putting God first in our lives. We recentered our lives around the only One who could save a marriage turned to ashes. We knew He was the only One who could keep our relationship strong. And He is the only One who can keep your marriage strong as well.

Thomas

On our fifteenth anniversary, I wanted to make one of Lysandra's dreams come true. I took her on a trip to Prince Edward Island, where *Anne of Green Gables* is set. We didn't have a lot of money, and we knew that the only way we could afford this trip was to sleep in our van. We took all the back seats out, put the full-size mattress from our guest room in the back, threw our suitcases in, and were off on our adventure.

This trip was one of the best memories from our twenty years of marriage. We would travel until we were too tired to travel anymore. We'd stop at a rest stop or gas station, crawl in the back of the van, put up the screens we'd fashioned out of sun protectors, and go to sleep. The next day we'd wake up and explore the area or drive until we came upon something interesting. It was a real adventure, and we were totally in sync. No fighting or frustrations, just fun and laughter with my best friend.

After fifteen years of marriage and much counseling of other couples, we had learned a thing or two about marriage. We knew we wanted to seek Christ. Lysandra would read the Bible to me each morning as I drove, we'd discuss our relationship, and we would take turns praying.

While on this trip, our close friend Evan gave us a book by Francis and Lisa Chan entitled *You and Me Forever*. Lysandra read that book out loud on our trip and I think it helped solidify the new focus we were trying to keep in our relationship. It verbalized the way we were living, a healthier God-centered relationship. We no longer looked at our fairy tale as a story where I'm happy forever because I always get my way and my spouse lives to fulfill all my wishes.

The new focus became a story where I want to live my life to please Jesus, and my marriage will be great because He will make it great. Listen to these words for Francis and Linda Chan: "*Many people will tell you to focus on your marriage, to focus on each other; but we discovered focusing on God's mission made our marriage amazing.*"[3] "*Without a healthy fear of God, we will not fully enjoy life and love. Without it our priorities will be completely off. Yet, if a healthy fear of God is at the foundation of who we are, a beautiful life and marriage can be built on this.*"[4]

Our marriage was strengthened during that trip. We took time for one another. We took time to focus on God. We prayed that God would be the center of our relationship and that He would be first. We began to discuss how we could help each other achieve their full potential for Jesus rather than how I could make her happy or how she could make me happy?

The Unpopular Truth

The truth is found in Scripture. It is true yet most unpopular. The truth is that your marriage isn't about your happiness. Your story isn't written with you as the hero or heroine. Your life was never meant to be about you. Your marriage was never meant to be about you. Your story is about Him. The Apostle Paul sums it up nicely in Galatians 2:20–21:

> *I have been crucified with Christ. It is no longer I who live, but Christ who lives in me. And the life I now live in the flesh I live by faith in the Son of God, who loved me and gave himself for me. I do not nullify the grace of God, for if righteousness were through the law, then Christ died for no purpose.*

Your aim in life ought to be to please God, not yourself. At all times you are to make it your goal to please God in every aspect of your life. This applies to your marriage too.

Often it seems easier to seek to please God at church, at work, with our service to Him, or with our friendships than it is to please God in our marriage relationship. Pleasing God with the way we treat our spouse is usually the last thing on our minds.

The Plot Twist

It's not too late for you to rewrite your definition of fairy tale. You may have been married for twenty years like us, are just starting out in year one, or have us all beat with fifty years of marriage under your belt. The number of years that you've been seeking for your own happiness in marriage doesn't matter. You can write a plot twist today in which you completely surprise everyone!

You can change the direction of your story by changing your focus to please God.

Here's how you can rewrite the story:
- Pray together for God to help you see where you aren't pleasing Him in your marriage relationship.
- Commit to one another to stop trying to seek your own happiness or make each other happy but rather to please God.
- Begin to seek Him first above all else.
- Memorize 2 Corinthians 5:9: *"So whether we are at home or away, we make it our aim to please Him."*
- Look for opportunities every day to please God.
- Encourage and support your spouse as they seek to please God.

Living the New Fairy Tale

What does this new fairy tale actually look like in real life? It's easy to say, "I'm turning over a new leaf; from now on I'm going to seek God not my own happiness." It's not so easy to live it out. Real life comes in and our flesh is strong. We want what we want when we want it. The only way we can truly live in a way that pleases Him is in the power of the Holy Spirit.

We look at the Apostle Paul as one of the greatest Christians to ever live, and yet look what he says about himself in Romans 7:18–19: *"For I know that nothing good dwells in me, that is, in my flesh. For I have the desire to do what is right, but not the ability to carry it out. For I do not do the good I want, but the evil I do not want is what I keep on doing."*

He knew what he wanted to do but found it impossible to do it. And the things that he never wanted to do are exactly the things that he found himself doing.

It's impossible for us in our own strength. Don't forget, we serve the God who can do the impossible. Remember what Jesus said in Matthew 19:26: *"But Jesus looked at them and said, 'With man this is impossible, but with God all things are possible.'"*

In the power of God's Holy Spirit, you have the ability to rewrite your definition of fairy tale. With His divine help you have the power to seek for God rather than seek for your own happiness. We can only succeed in the power of God because our flesh is so strong, and our spirit is weak.

The Apostle Paul continues to write about the power of our flesh in Galatians 5:17: *"For the desires of the flesh are against the Spirit, and the desires of the Spirit are against the flesh, for these are opposed to each other, to keep you from doing the things you want to do."*

When you're tempted to go after that thing you believe will bring you happiness, you must stop and ask God, "Will this word or action please *You* or *me*?" When the answer is that both you and God will be pleased by this word or action, that's awesome. Go for it. But many times, what pleases God and what pleases you are two different things. That's when you must choose His way. You must depend upon His Holy Spirit to help you choose the right path.

Remember the illustration of a husband and wife chasing their own happiness in marriage from Chapter One? As each chased their own happiness on their own course, the couple moved in opposite directions. The longer they lived this way, the further away from one another they got.

But here we see this new way of living where the husband and the wife have rewritten their definition of fairy tale. Their fairy tale is now defined by two people seeking to please God. This couple is two people walking toward God rather than toward their own happiness. Because they're both pursuing God, they are walking the same path together, traveling the same direction. They stay close to one another as they move closer to God.

Lysandra

I never felt this battle between pursuing God and pursuing my own happiness more than when Thomas received a job offer in Alabama. We were serving in Iowa at the time. I was quite content with where we were and how our lives were going. Our four daughters were growing up with both sets of grandparents nearby. Our girls had girl cousins their age who were their best friends from both sides of our families living just down the street. We lived in a nice home. We had a great support system in our church family. Life was good.

Then everything was turned upside down when a church called Thomas to be their pastor. This would mean a move out of state. It would mean tearing our girls away from their home and family. This move would mean leaving our church family just as we were seeing growth and progress.

My happiness appeared to be found right where we were. I didn't want to go. I was certain it was the wrong decision.

We talked it over for several days, we prayed about it constantly, we fasted, and we asked God to show us the right path to take. Thomas told me, "We are moving. I know it's what we're supposed to do."

I cried. I told him I disagreed with his decision. I thought God wanted us to stay where we were.

If I were still chasing my own happiness, the scene would have played out like this:

"No! I'm not going. I refuse to rip my children away from everything they know and love to move across the country just because you want to. If you go, you go without me and the girls."

By this time, I was past the point of pursuing my own happiness in marriage. I had seen God take care of me and my children in beautiful ways in the past, and I trusted Him now as well. I was seeking to please Him not myself. I understood it pleased God when I followed my husband's lead, so I said to Thomas through my tears, "Okay, I'll move with you even though I don't think it's the right choice, and I'll work like crazy in our next ministry."

The next day, I began to go through the house and make piles to take to Goodwill and piles for trash. I gathered boxes and began to pack up those items which we wouldn't need in the next month. I set my eyes on our next ministry and began to internally say goodbye to this one. I cried a lot, but I was willing.

This is what it means to seek to please God rather than self. It means in those scary, dark moments you choose to do what's right even if you don't want to, even if you believe it will make you miserable. You trust the promises of God. You put your faith in seeking God rather than believing in your own pursuit of happiness.

Thomas

For me this scenario looked a lot different. I too was seeking God first. I too wanted to make the right decision for my wife, my daughters, my current church family, and my future church family. I wanted to seek God over my own happiness. That meant I had to follow the leading of His Spirit even though my wife didn't want to go and might resent me for it.

I was scared too. Moving was the hard choice, not the easy

one. When I came to Lysandra and told her I knew we needed to move, I could see how devastated she was. But I wasn't seeking to please my wife but God. I believed this was how I was to please Him at that moment.

It was one week after making the decision to move that God totally changed my heart. He showed me we weren't supposed to move but stay exactly where we were. I called my wife immediately. I said, "Lysandra, we aren't moving. God has shown me we're to stay here." She was relieved and thanked me for listening to God's leading.

God was showing both of us something different at the same time to see if we were seeking Him, pleasing each other, or chasing our own happiness. He wanted our whole hearts. Would we listen even if we weren't on the same page?

Seeking the Author

God taught us both something through that experience. He taught us that when we both seek Him first, everything else will turn out fine. The marriage will be fine, the kids will be fine, the finances will be fine. When we seek Him first, all those things will be taken care of, just as Matthew 6:33 says: *"But seek first the kingdom of God and his righteousness, and all these things will be added to you."*

Putting God first is the only way to true joy and happiness. Seeking to please Him is always the best plan. Your marriage will be better than you ever imagined when you redefine the fairy tale from me being happy to me pleasing God. Let go of the story you thought you'd be living and find joy in the story God has written for you.

King Solomon made it so clear when he wrote in Proverbs 16:7: *"When a man's ways please the Lord, he makes even his enemies to be at peace with him."*

We can testify to this truth. When we stopped seeking our

own happiness and began pursuing God with all our hearts and pleasing Him, our marriage relationship changed. We had more joy and a lot more peace. Our relationship is what we always wanted it to be. It happened when we stopped striving for it and started seeking God first.

Making God's Plan Our Purpose

Seeking God and pursuing His plan must become our purpose if we want to live a fulfilled life and reach our full potential. We are not only seeking God ourselves, but also encouraging our spouse to seek God and draw close to Him so that they will live a fulfilled life and reach their full potential. When a married couple seeks God together, the relationship that's born is astonishingly deeper, closer, more peaceful, and more joyful.

Here are some practical ways to seek God in your marriage relationship:

- Pray regularly together.
- Talk about God together.
- Worship together.
- Serve together.
- Praise together.
- Study God's Word together.
- Share how God's working in your life together.
- Spend time with other godly couples together.
- Plan generous giving together.
- Spend quality time in God's creation together.

Stop right now, pray together, commit to make seeking God your new purpose, and watch a true fairy tale be created in your lives.

3

Disenchanted

Setting Unreasonable Expectations

Once upon a time . . . there lived a boy and girl who were disenchanted.

Thomas

If you asked twenty-two-year-old me if I had expectations going into marriage, I would have answered without hesitation—*no*. The weird thing about expectations is they are in our minds when we don't know they're there. I didn't understand that I had expectations going into our marriage twenty years ago. Now, after maturing, growing, studying, counseling, and self-reflecting, I realize I had expectations that I was unaware of.

Looking back now, I can honestly tell you that I only had three expectations of my future wife—time, food, and sex, and not necessarily in that order. I expected that I would get to be with the girl that I loved a lot. I wasn't naïve enough to think that we would spend every waking hour together, but I wanted most of her time. I figured once we were finally married, we'd spend all but eight hours a weekday together and of course all our weekends together.

You have to understand, I pursued Lysandra for seven years. I waited a long time to get her undivided attention, and I expected it to be great! Before we got married, I went off to college in Florida while she was back in Iowa, and it was terrible to be so far removed from her. I was certain that after we said "I do" it meant together forever. I expected her time.

I also didn't realize that I expected her to cook for me. People always make the joke about guys that want a mom, not a wife. My mom didn't cook for me very often, so for me, I wanted a wife who would cook for me. Not only cook for me but cook what I wanted and how I wanted it cooked. Lysandra is an awesome cook! Before we got married, she would cook for me at her parents' house or mine. I loved her cooking, and I expected that she would always cook for me after we got married.

I most definitely expected sex, and I expected it often. We were both virgins when we got married so that was the activity that I most looked forward to on our wedding night and the rest of our nights. I expected both of us to want sex, enjoy sex, think about sex, and have sex often. I didn't know this was an expectation at the time, it was just there in my mind. I thought about how great it would be to be able to touch this girl that I loved any time that I wanted.

These were my expectations going into marriage, and it didn't take long to figure out that my marriage would not be everything that I expected it to be. Just one short week after the honeymoon, reality set in, and I became disenchanted.

Lysandra

If I share all the expectations that I had twenty years ago, right before I walked down the aisle, I think it could fill up all this book and a second one. I expected a lot! There were some expectations that I knew I had. In fact, I had a list written in my notebook. This was my checklist of what I wanted in a husband. Did any of you have a checklist of what you wanted in a spouse, or was it just me?

I had witnessed girls close to me settle for a subpar husband when they deserved so much better. They could have had much higher standards, but they fell in love with a mediocre guy. I wanted to make sure that didn't happen to me, so I wrote a list of nonnegotiable items. If the guy didn't meet these criteria, I'd make sure that I didn't get too close to him and "accidentally" fall in love.

Here are the top items that were on my list:
- He must have a personal relationship with Jesus.
- He must be walking close to Jesus.
- He must treat his mother well.
- He must make me laugh.
- He must be attractive.

Yes, I actually wrote *be attractive*. I love Jesus, but I'm still human! These were my known expectations before marriage. I dated Thomas for many years, even though I could see he didn't check the second box and unbeknownst to me he didn't check the first box either until he was almost nineteen years old. By the time he proposed to me, he checked all the boxes and was an expectation come true. I knew that I could say *yes*.

These expectations weren't the problem though. It was the unknown expectations that destroyed our fairy tale. I'll share a few of the numerous unknown expectations that I had deep in my heart.

I expected Thomas to love me and act loving toward me

100% of the time. I expected him to put me first in everything. I expected to be happy in marriage. I expected him to appreciate me. I expected him to notice me physically every day and every time that I changed an outfit, which is way too often. I expected him to want sex more than I wanted it. I expected him to clean up after himself. I expected him to buy me small birthday presents, Christmas presents, anniversary presents, and *just because* presents. I expected him to follow God closely all the time. I expected him to be the spiritual leader in our family. I expected him to talk to me and share feelings. I expected him to protect me and provide for me. I expected him to ask and value my opinion. I expected him to try to make me happy every day.

This is not an exhaustive list! I actually feel sorry for the guy as I examine my original plethora of expectations. One by one, Thomas missed the mark of every single one of my expectations. I didn't know these were present in my heart until after we got married, when I became disenchanted.

Hidden Expectations

You too have expectations, whether you realize it or not. Like something from a Stephen King novel, they are there lurking in the dark corners of your mind just waiting to destroy your fairy tale. Even if you are the most easygoing, relaxed person to ever get married, you expect some things out of your spouse.

You most likely have some rather obvious known expectations that are reasonable for every spouse to look forward to. You reasonably expect your spouse to love you, to care about you, to like you, and to be faithful to you both emotionally and physically. In fact, you probably listed some of those expectations in your marriage vows and promised to do those things on your wedding day.

Most traditional wedding vows go something like this:

I, (Name), take you, (Name) to be my lawfully wedded
wife/husband.
To have and to hold from this day forward.
For better, for worse.
For richer, for poorer.
In sickness and in health.
So long as we both shall live.
Until death do us part.

Reasonable expectations aren't the culprit in destroying your fairy tale, it's those other expectations, the unreasonable ones. Often the unreasonable expectations we hold our spouse to are the unknown, hidden ones. It's those sneaky ones that you didn't even know that you had. I expect you to play with our kids every day after work. I expect you to say I love you and kiss me goodbye before you leave the house. I expect you to want to play board games with my family once a week. I expect you to enjoy sex. I expect you to agree with my political positions. I expect you to listen to my opinions. I expect you to cook a homemade meal every night by six. I expect you to say thank you when I fill up the car with gas.

Not all unreasonable expectations are bad. On the contrary, most of them are very good. But to expect someone to be perfect is unreasonable. It's important to identify and bring your unknown expectations to light. It's much easier to understand why you're frustrated with your spouse for not measuring up if you understand what's on the measuring tape.

In her book *Marriage: To Have and to Hold*, June Hunt describes the negative effect unreasonable expectations can have on your relationship.

> *When unrealistic expectations reside in marriage and those expectations aren't met, couples can turn to certain counterfeits for a false sense of comfort. How easy to get*

caught in the trap of focusing on "whatever meets my needs" that can lead to expecting others to "do whatever I want them to do."

And who better to do that than the mate who at one time caught our eye? We think we've entered the storybook tale of "Happily ever after." But then reality hits! We keep expecting from our spouse what we can't get. We think our empty bucket will now be filled and stay forever full. "This is what I expect you to do for me."

But our bucket has holes in it-holes that no person can fill. Our unrealistic expectations are founded on faulty assumptions-not words of wisdom. We are deceived and don't even know it.[5]

The Harsh Reality

That perfect scenario of prince and princess living in eternal perfection isn't reality. No one can meet all your expectations. Setting unreasonable expectations will destroy your fairy tale. You want that happily ever after but your unreasonable expectations, whether they be known or unknown, are ruining it.

When you set these unrealistic expectations for your spouse, you set them up to be the villain of your marriage. You make them the hideous troll under the bridge who destroys your happiness because, no matter how hard they try, they can't be everything that you expect them to be. Your expectations set your spouse up for failure, and you set yourself up for disappointment, resentment, and disenchantment.

You have expectations of your spouse. You may not know it, but you do. The expectations you have create a life of discontentment and discouragement.

Whatever year of marriage you may be in right now, do some self-examination to figure out what your expectations are. Don't just do a quick thought but really dig deep. What's at least one unknown expectation you have for your spouse? An expectation you have, but you never really thought about before. It could be as simple as expecting him to put the toilet seat down or to cuddle for a bit after sex. It could be as trivial as expecting her to put the garage door down after she parks the car or watch a movie with you once and a while.

Thomas

I forced Lysandra to be the troll under the bridge with one of my unrealistic expectations. It was in years one and two of our marriage. I expected Lysandra to respect me enough to wait for me to fix things. She would have a list of broken items or house repairs for her dad to accomplish when he came to visit. My ego was wounded. I got so mad that she went around me and had her dad fix *my* house. She was demeaning me. I felt emasculated.

I also expected Lysandra not to nag me about repairing things that I hadn't fixed yet. There was no way for her to win. I forced her to be the evil troll. She couldn't bug me about fixing things, she couldn't ask her dad to fix things, and back then, she couldn't fix things herself. My expectations of her were completely unreasonable. It wasn't fair. And to be honest, the real culprit in this scenario was my own personal pride. I didn't and still don't know how to repair most things, but I was too proud to admit that to my bride. I was also too proud to let someone else come into my house and fix anything, because I thought that's what I was supposed to be doing.

I wish I hadn't behaved this way; I do regret it. However, because I never fixed anything Lysandra took things into her own hands. Now she can fix almost anything, build anything, and YouTube her way to repair most of our house. I take credit for that.

Lysandra

Being on the other end of those expectations was really miserable. I remember our first cozy home in Foley, Alabama, on Orange Court. It was this picturesque brick home on a cul-de-sac in a quiet neighborhood. I loved that house, but like any home, things would break and need repairing.

One time when my parents came for a visit, we had a wooden dining-room chair that was broken. Two of the wooden spokes had splintered and needed repairing. At the time I had no idea how to fix splintered wood nor did we have the money to buy supplies. To my knowledge, YouTube didn't exist, at least it didn't to me. While Thomas was at work, my parents took me grocery shopping. It was always an exciting time because we had no money, and when my parents came, they would let me buy meat. We almost never ate meat back then because we couldn't afford it. While we were out, my dad asked if there was anything that he could repair on their visit? I excitedly said, "Yes! The dining room chairs!"

We picked up some wood glue and came home to fix the chairs. I was eagerly assisting my father repair the chairs when Thomas came home. I said, "Hi, Honey!" and gave him a big hug.

He didn't hug me back. In a suspicious tone he asked, "What are you guys doing?"

I replied happily, "My dad's fixing the chairs."

Thomas said nothing. He walked into our bedroom. It was obvious that I had upset him. I felt nervous, my heart was pounding, and I followed him into the bedroom. We began to whisper fight. You know how those fights sound. You can't fight too loud because there's someone right outside the door or down the hall. It went something like this . . .

"Why are you mad?"

"I told you I'd fix those chairs. Why would you go against me and have your dad do it? You're showing me that you don't respect me!"

"I'm sorry, I didn't know you wanted to fix the chairs. Do you want me to go tell him to stop?"

"No, but don't have him fix anything else in *my* house."

"Okay, I won't. I didn't know. Will you forgive me?"

"Yes. I forgive you."

He still sounded a little mad, but I accepted the forgiveness and walked out of our bedroom with a big smile attempting to overcompensate for the obvious fight that we just had. I wanted my parents to think everything was fine like we never fought.

I had missed the mark of Thomas's expectations; I failed him. His expectations made me a failure.

Life Is Unpredictable

Expectations don't factor in the unpredictability of life. We set known and unknown expectations and hold onto them for years. But situations change, people change, and life is unpredictable. You can't possibly know what's coming around every corner. Sometimes your expectations which were once reasonable become unreasonable when life changes.

You can't expect your spouse to do the chores they did at the beginning of your marriage forever. It's unreasonable to expect your spouse to perform sexually for the rest of their life the way they did when you first got married. You can't expect your spouse to spend the same amount of quality time with you after children as they did before children. It's unrealistic to expect your spouse to help around the house during a busy work season in the same way as they did before they got a promotion.

Life is always changing. Seasons come and go. There are so many variables to our lives. Expectations that were once reasonable may become unreasonable due to the changes in your day-to-day. For you to set your expectations and refuse to change them is villainous.

Lysandra

My expectations were set. They were high. They were unknown. They caused so much damage in our relationship. I wanted perfection, was that so much to ask?

I didn't understand that life would change, and my expectations would need to change with the seasons. One of the times this became evident was when Thomas began to understand he struggled with depression. Neither of us understood the vastness of its reach in our marriage.

My expectation of his sex drive had to change with this new season. From before our marriage, I had expected him to be fully and almost obsessively interested in me sexually. Suddenly around year twelve he didn't seem to initiate sex anymore. He seemed less and less interested in me physically. It seemed he no longer noticed me.

I did what any normal woman would do, I accused him of an affair. I said, "You're no longer attracted to me because I'm so fat that you went out and found someone younger and skinnier than me. I know you're cheating on me!"

He denied having an affair and tried his best to convince me he still found me attractive. I refused to believe him. My unrealistic, unchanging expectations destroyed our fairy tale. They created a spiral of hurt and failure. I was hurt that he didn't meet the expectations I had set twelve years ago. He was made a failure because he couldn't keep up with his younger, healthier self. I created all this turmoil because I couldn't see my expectations needed to change.

I couldn't understand that we were in a new season. I couldn't accept the different lifestyle we needed to have for this season. My expectations stayed rigid and unmovable.

Thomas

I felt the biggest impact of season change when we had our first baby. Remember, one of my three expectations for marriage was all the time we would enjoy together. We moved all the way from Iowa to Florida when we first got married. Lysandra didn't know anyone but me. It was great. She spent all her time with me when she wasn't working.

She went off to work in the morning, I went to school, and we would be home at night together. Weekends were spent serving in a church just over the border in Foley, Alabama. We did absolutely everything together when we weren't at work or school. Every evening while at home, she would rub my head. We would lie in bed and watch movies together. She would cook for me, and we'd eat together. I had her full attention. Then, after two short years of marriage, the babies came and ruined it all!

Our new season started two and a half years after our wedding. Kathryne Marie was born. She was the only person that I knew that was more selfish than I was. She wanted to eat all the time, she cried for my wife's attention, and she was so needy! She stole my wife.

My expectations for my wife's time were no longer being met. Rather than lying in bed watching movies, Lysandra was nursing our baby. Lysandra could no longer give me her full attention each evening. She was busy bathing our daughter and tucking her into bed. I didn't like it. I was forced to change my expectations of our time together.

My expectations could not stay the same as they were at the beginning of our marriage after we had children. Expectations become unreasonable when they are unchanging with the seasons of life.

Don't Get Stuck in the Expectation Rut

When you have an expectation in marriage that begins when you say "I do" and never ends or changes, you're stuck in an expectation rut.

In their book *Everybody Fights*, Penn and Kim Holderness describe expectations as secret contracts. *"Secret contracts are the silent deals you make with your partner by default and through routine. They are tasks we take on and identities we assume with an invisible handshake at the start of a relationship that we continue-till death do us part."*[6]

Expectations that are set and kept through all different seasons of life and busyness are probably not set intentionally. At one point one spouse expects something of another, and that expectation becomes like a secret contract for years. Expectation ruts aren't healthy. These ruts can destroy your fairy tale.

Unmet Expectations

If you have high unreasonable expectations like we did in the beginning of our marriage, you will most assuredly have unmet expectations. You will be disappointed, and you will become disenchanted.

King Solomon was the wisest man to ever live, and he had this to say about disappointment and its effect on us in Proverbs 13:12: *"Hope deferred makes the heart sick, but a desire fulfilled is a tree of life."* The pain of disappointment can last a long time and change the way that you view people and situations.

The damage caused by unrealistic expectations is directly related to how passionate you are about having the expectation met. The more passionate, the more damage done.

If you are overly passionate about the expectation you have for your spouse to change the oil in the car before it hits 5,000 miles, then you're going to be so angry when they forget or get too busy to do it. Lashing out in anger, you will most likely say words you shouldn't say and hurt them deeply. The damage is done.

If you're extremely passionate about an expectation for your spouse to remember to buy you presents for special occasions, you have placed yourself on a road to dissatisfaction. You're going to be terribly disappointed every time they forget a present or fail to get you a meaningful gift. You will set yourself up for deep hurt and set them up for failure. Both spouses begin to resent each other. The damage is done.

Expectations create a false hope of happiness in our relationships. The more passionate you are about your expectations, the higher they are set, and the more unreasonable your expectations are, the more your hope will come crashing down when your spouse inevitably does not meet them. Unreasonable expectations will destroy your fairy tale.

4

Set the Prisoner Free

Releasing Unreasonable Expectations

Once upon a time . . . a girl freed a boy from the prison of her expectations.

Lysandra

I didn't mean to create a prison for Thomas. I didn't know that I had. I honestly thought I was just expecting basic, reasonable, realistic behaviors out of him. I didn't understand that all the parameters and guidelines I wanted him to follow in our marriage became a cold, stone-walled prison I had built.

Tearing down the prison of my expectations proved to be more difficult than I thought it would be. When we got married, Thomas agreed it would be his job to take the trash out—like forever. He would take the trash out every time it got full. My expectation was set. I didn't believe it would ever need to change.

In year one of our marriage the trash at the apartment had to be taken across the parking lot. I don't remember much about the trash at the apartment, which means that he must have met the expectation there. I remember the trash at our first home. We moved just across the border from Florida into Alabama.

Our first house was a dream come true for me. I loved it. It was so cute and pretty. It was red brick with a white porch across the front, blue shutters on the windows, and the most beautiful old oak tree in the back yard. My job was to take care of the house—the dishes, the grocery shopping, the laundry, the bathrooms, the cooking, the cleaning, and the minor repairs. Thomas had two jobs. Mowing and taking trash out. We both worked full time. I felt he was getting a bargain. I felt that my expectations were fair, balanced, and reasonable.

Thomas agreed to these terms. He was cool with each of our chore lists. Yet, for some reason, he couldn't seem to keep up his end of the deal. The trash was constantly overflowing nearly all the time, and the yard was so long that our retired neighbor mowed it for us because he was tired of looking at it. This was uncomfortable not only because my twenty-three-year-old husband should have been mowing our yard rather than our sixty-something neighbor, but also because our neighbor mowed it shirtless, wearing only tan hiking boots and the shortest cutoff denim shorts I'd ever seen!

I was angry with my new husband. My expectations were not being met. These were the expectations he agreed to. We had company often; we ran the youth group together and had teens over frequently. Later, we had babies with diaper waste. The trash filled repeatedly throughout the week. It filled up nearly every day. I would remind him, "The trash is full." He would say, "Okay, I'll take it out."

He would go back to watching TV, playing video games, working on his computer, or whatever he was doing. The trash sat there rotting. I would cook, throw the wrappers or food scraps in the trash, and watch them fall all over the kitchen floor. I'd get so angry!

"With everything I do in this house, serving him every day, he can't just take the trash out?" I would huff and puff and take it out myself, slamming the door behind me.

This exact scenario played out for the next ten years. There would be periodic explosions when the trash wars would come to a head. I'd lose it on him, he'd apologize, take out the trash for three days, and then go back to normal again. It was a prison of unmet expectations.

One sunny summer day I was cooking lunch. I went to throw away the vegetable ends and scraps. I turned to the trash; it was full as usual. This time I didn't get mad; this time I cried. I cried to God.

I said, "God, I will no longer expect Thomas to take out the trash. I will do this chore to serve my husband. I won't tell him, guilt him, or shame him. I won't slam the door. I will quietly take out the trash, even if I do it for the rest of our lives together."

I held the trash can up in the air like a crazy person and submitted my expectations for the trash to God. I broke down the prison walls of expectations. I became happier, and Thomas became more carefree.

Eventually our little babies became little girls. Pro-marriage tip: Change from a large kitchen trash bin to a mini-bin with grocery store sacks for trash bags. It will fill up much more frequently, but your children can carry the little bags out, and as a bonus you'll be recycling all those grocery bags you use.

Thomas

You guys, I tried! I promise, I tried to take the trash out. I honestly wanted to do that for my wife. It just filled up so fast. I swear I would be walking a bag to the outside bin and by the time I got back inside the trash can would be full again. I couldn't keep up with it. I failed my wife's expectations repeatedly for years.

When Lysandra dropped her expectation of me to take care of the trash, life became really peaceful. I started to notice Lysandra hadn't asked me to take out the trash for a while. If I saw her taking the trash out, I would take it out of her hands and take it the rest of the way. It wasn't long before I began taking the trash out on my own.

Her expectation for me to take out the trash wasn't unreasonable in and of itself. It was unrealistic, however, for me at that stage of my maturity. When she released me from that expectation, we were both happier.

I'm happy to report that the trash wars have ended, and I now have an app on my phone to remind me to take the trash out. I almost never miss our two trash days each week. We're both a lot happier now.

Is This Expectation Reasonable or Unreasonable?

It's not wrong to have expectations in marriage. It's wrong to set unreasonable expectations for your spouse. But what makes an expectation reasonable or unreasonable?

Unrealistic expectations are expectations which cannot be met, whether they cannot be met because the person is not mature enough, not physically able, not emotionally ready to do so, or the season of life makes the expectation impossible to meet. Expectations that were reasonable at the beginning of your marriage may have become unreasonable over time. In the same way, expectations that were unrealistic in the beginning of your marriage may have become realistic.

It is healthy to examine your expectations frequently. Ask yourself questions like, "What am I expecting my spouse to do?" "Is it reasonable for me to ask this of my spouse at this present time in their life?" "How am I expecting my spouse to make me feel?"

Realistic Expectations:

- I expect complete faithfulness—emotionally and physically.
- I expect kindness as the norm.
- I expect honesty.
- I expect respect.

Unrealistic Expectations:

- I expect my spouse to make me feel loved.
- I expect my spouse to make me happy.
- I expect my spouse to meet all my needs.
- I expect my spouse to fulfill all my wants.
- I expect my spouse to anticipate my desires.

Free the Captives

Releasing your expectations frees you and frees your spouse. When you release your spouse from your expectations, you free yourself from continuous hurt. You free your spouse from being a constant failure. When you release your spouse from unreasonable expectations, you free them from being the villainous monster of your marriage. You destroy the chill of rigid prison walls and bring in the warmth and freedom of peace and contentment.

Be free! Let go of the expectations. Like Elsa tells us, "Let it go, let it go." Now you will be singing that song all day long. You're welcome! Let go of the expectations that your spouse will make you happy, make you feel loved, help you with everything you want, remember every anniversary, initiate sex, say the words you want to hear, spend money the way you want, or spend a certain amount of time with you. Let it all go.

The first step in letting go of your unreasonable expectations is to identify them. What are your unmet expectations of your spouse? If you aren't sure, we have an easy way to help you figure them out. Think of the thing or things they do or don't do that make you mad. What do they do that gets on your nerves? What are they not doing that you wish they would do? Those are your unmet expectations.

Write a list of your unmet expectations of your spouse. Identify them. Accept them as a loss you're grieving. You can be sad over unmet expectations. You can grieve the loss. Just don't stay there. Have the funeral and say goodbye. Then walk away from the casket. Your spouse will never be that, do that, or meet that desire. Mourn the loss. Understand that if you indulge in the sorrow of the loss, it will hold you and your spouse captive in a prison of disappointment and anger.

Take that expectation that has imprisoned you and your spouse and hold it up to God. Tell Him you release it to Him. Confess your pursuit of happiness rather than Him and release it. Ask Him to free you from it. Ask Him to break the chains, destroy the prison walls, and create the fairy tale He wants for you.

Now it's time to communicate with your spouse. Share the expectation you are letting go of. Tell them, "I release you from this expectation."

The conversation may go something like this. "I've been holding you to an unreasonable expectation. I've been expecting you to remember our anniversary on your own. Because of this expectation I've set, I feel hurt and undervalued when you forget. I realize this isn't something you can remember at this stage in your life. I understand you may never be able to remember our anniversaries. I want you to know I'm releasing you from all anniversaries. I no longer expect you to remember the day we had our first date, the day we got engaged, or the day we got married. If I want to celebrate, I'll plan something special and get you a gift."

It may feel like you lost. It may feel like you are sacrificing greatly. The truth is you just won. You freed yourself. You freed your spouse. You will both now benefit from the absence of this expectation. Rest in the freedom of released expectations.

Thomas

There was a time when I couldn't imagine releasing Lysandra from my time expectations. Early on I made it clear to her that she needed to check with me before making plans . . . with anyone . . . ever. This was an unreasonable expectation I had for her for several years.

If she wanted to go out with her sister, she had to ask me first. If she wanted to go to her mom's house, she had to check with me. If she wanted to meet with a woman at church to counsel, she had to get my permission. I didn't see it as unreasonable; I saw it as respect and consideration.

The truth is that it was unreasonable. It was a high expectation I set for her so that my desire for time with her would be protected. Lysandra was good about calling me first most of the time. If she didn't, I would get upset. I would tell her, "You should have checked with me first. You're not respecting me when you just go off." I had created a prison, and I had no idea that's what I was doing. Like Rapunzel's "mother," I locked her away in a tower.

It all changed when I saw it in another man. I saw another husband controlling his wife's time. If she went to spend time with her family, he got mad and made her pay for it later by giving her the silent treatment or yelling at her. There were times she counted the cost and went anyway because she so deeply wanted to be a part of her extended family.

I wasn't that bad, but I saw the similarities. After that, when Lysandra would ask me if she could go to her mom's house on Thursday, I would answer, "Sure, if you want to. Have fun." When she asked me if she could spend the day helping her sister, I would say, "Of course, but I'll miss you."

I began texting her while she was away and telling her, "Have fun. You deserve this time with your sister."

I kept one expectation; I asked her to have a frozen pizza in the freezer if she was going to be gone all day. She almost always has easy food ready for me to eat or pop in the oven when she's gone. Now, the prison walls are totally broken down. She goes wherever she wants and does whatever she wants. We talk every night about the next day. I ask, "What do you have on the schedule tomorrow?" We compare our calendars, and we schedule times for each other just like we do for other appointments.

We're both so much happier now. We enjoy our time together. We enjoy the freedom in our relationship.

Lysandra

Although I never felt like a prisoner to Thomas's expectations, when I think back to the way things used to be, I know I'd never want to go back to it. Life is so much better now that we operate the way we do with our calendars. We have mutual respect and consideration for one another.

We both check with one another before making plans that affect both of us. We also share what we have going on with the other, so they are in the loop and know where we are and what's happening.

Now it's about consideration, not expectations.

The Opposite of Expectations is Contentment

If you have released your spouse from your expectations, you have brought in a beautiful time of contentment. You have now chosen to be pleased with the life you have and the spouse you are married to.

We are encouraged by June Hunt in her book *Marriage: To Have and to Hold*. She says, *"Instead of living with unrealistic*

3. Talk _____.

Talk It Over

1. Talk about any sexual experiences from your past that you need to share with your spouse.

2. Talk about how often you would like to have sex each week.

3. Talk about what kind of affirmation would help you during sex.

4. Talk about your favorite part of foreplay.

5. Talk about what you would like to change about your sexual relationship in the future.

FIGHTING IN YOUR MARRIAGE
FOR YOUR MARRIAGE

Session 2: Fighting For Great Sex

Intro:

1. Talk _Communicate Before_

2. Talk _Communicate Sharing During_

904-257-3062

4. Celebrate the _Small_ _____ Victories.

Ps 104: 1 - 4

5. Forgive, _remember_ _____, and Release.

Talk It Over

1. Talk about a wound that is still open.

2. Talk to God out loud and pray for healing for that wound.

3. Talk about the feelings that arise when you identify the wound.

4. Talk about the ways you see God working during the healing process.

5. Talk to God out loud praising for His working in your relationship.

FIGHTING IN YOUR MARRIAGE FOR YOUR MARRIAGE

Session 4: Fighting For Healing

Psalm 55:12

Psalm 55: 17-19, 22

Intro:

1. ___Identify___ the Wound.

2. Go to God ___Daily___ for Healing.

3. Regularly ___update___ Your Spouse on the Progression of the Wound.

Ps. 34:18

expectations regarding what you don't have, be grateful to God for what you do have."[7]

By letting go of your unreasonable expectations, you have become content, and there are a lot of benefits that come with finding contentment. The Apostle Paul put it this way in his first letter to Timothy in 1 Timothy 6:6: *"But godliness with contentment is great gain."* Contentment in marriage is great gain. It's lovely to enjoy each other without all these expectations hanging over your heads. If you haven't experienced it yet, it's time to let go of expectations and embrace contentment.

Release your unreasonable expectations, enjoy the freedom of contentment, and create your fairy tale.

5

Slay All the Dragons

Fighting Every Battle to Win

Once upon a time . . . there was a boy who tried to slay every dragon.

Thomas

I was tired. I worked hard all day. I just wanted to watch the Hawkeyes basketball game and play around on my iPad. It was my way of relaxing. As soon as I walked in the door Lysandra wanted me to talk to her, play with the girls, and help with discipline. I thought, "Can't you give me just five minutes? I'm tired!"

We had been married for four years, had two adorable little blonde baby girls and a third on the way. My expectant wife sat crying on the bed accusing me of not giving her and the girls enough attention. She said that she felt I was too busy with church work, and she was also unhappy with the way I spent my free time.

Looking back, I see how selfish I was, but at the time I was so worn out and tired. I felt attacked. I worked hard for our family and our church and when I got home, I needed some downtime. After giving myself all day to the people of our church, sermon preparation, and keeping a hundred-year-old church building from falling apart around us, I felt like it was fair for me to come home and relax a little bit.

The fight was on, and I was going into it with the mindset of Floyd Mayweather Jr. He retired from boxing with a record of 50 wins and no losses. There was no way that I was going to lose.

I viewed apologies as losses, so I wasn't even considering saying sorry. I love to win. I am a winner. I always win, and that night was no different. After a long enough argument, I had Lysandra apologizing to me. Yeah, I was that good. Really, I was that bad.

She deserved an apology from me. Even though I was tired and over worked, she was too. She worked in our church, cared for our girls, and took care of our entire house. She was worn out. She wanted me to help around the house, show her attention, and help with the girls. I should have been happy to support her. I was wrong, but in those early years, you would never hear me admit that.

I viewed every fight as a dragon to be slayed. Every fight that I won was a dragon that I conquered and a trophy that I hung on my wall. There was no fight that I would walk away from and nothing I wouldn't do to be victorious.

Lysandra

In the beginning of our marriage, it quickly became clear that I was supposed to lose all the fights. It seemed no matter the circumstances, our fights ended with me saying sorry. I remember thinking around our fourth month of marriage, "I know I'm not perfect, but how can I always be the only one who's wrong?"

I was used to losing. I was even comfortable losing. I was terrible at every sport and never won anything. As a little girl, I went out for tee ball one year. I was so bad that my entire team groaned with disappointment every time that I went up to bat. I didn't care; I played to have fun. I grew up in a family of happy losers. Most of our Gilchrist family weren't competitive in board games and weren't good in sports. Games were about fun. We laughed when we won, and we laughed when we lost.

We were happy this way. Our house was relaxingly calm; there weren't very many arguments while I was growing up. When there was an argument, it was talked out until all parties involved said "I'm sorry" and hugged it out.

When people in our family argued, there were no winners or losers, it was about resolution. Now there I was, newly married to a guy who wanted to fight every fight and, most importantly, needed to win every battle. He wanted to slay every dragon and it was destroying our fairy tale.

Thomas

My home was totally different. We were winners. We all played multiple sports and were very athletic and extremely competitive. We all played games to win, and not just to win, but to slaughter the opponent. Then we would sing loudly in the loser's face, "I'm the winner, I'm the winner. The W-I-N-N-E-R. I'm the one that did the best, I'm the one that beat all the rest. I'm the winner, I'm the winner. The W-I-N-N-E-R."

My family and I always wanted to win. One of our mottos was, "If you don't win, why are you playing?" Another favorite phrase in my home was, "If you're not cheating, then you're not trying." It was win at all costs in my house, and the bigger the win, the better. This applied to sports, cards, competitions, and arguments.

I didn't know we were excessively competitive until Lysandra expressed astonishment when she came to my house for supper and games while we were dating. My little brother Jonathan is seventeen years younger than I am. Jonathan was around four or five at the time. We ate supper, then got out Candy Land to play on the floor with my cute little brother Jonathan. I played to win, while Lysandra was slipping Jonathan the cards he needed.

Even with her help, Jonathan could not defeat me. I creamed him! I got up, danced around singing the winner's song, and shamed him in true Osterkamp fashion. My little brother ran up the stairs crying while my mom and I laughed at him. Lysandra was watching the scene in disbelief.

Lysandra

Sometimes I still can't believe I married this guy!

Thomas

I can't believe it either!

Lysandra

After that tragic scene between Thomas and his brother, I begged him to go up and apologize to Jonathan. Jonathan was the cutest kid; he had these big chubby cheeks and adorable smile. He would run to me and jump in my arms when I came over. I pleaded with Thomas, "Just go upstairs, tell him you're sorry. We can play another game and let him win."

He thought it was hilarious that I would even suggest this, laughed out loud, and said unapologetically, "No." I should have known I was marrying into a crazy family when his mom, who was listening in on our entire exchange, sat laughing on the couch, and said, "Jonathan's fine; he's got to learn!"

The signs were all there that Thomas was an obsessively competitive person. When we went to my family's house for a game night, this time the scene was reversed. Now he was on our territory. Yet it still ended in a fight and with me, as per usual, saying, "I'm sorry."

After dinner, we got out our 2001 favorite family game; it was Taboo. We loved that game. We played it all the time. Now Thomas was with my family entering into a traditional Gilchrist game night. We divided into teams and began the "competition."

My dad and Thomas were on a team. This may have been our first mistake. When the opposing team got stuck on a word, my dad would make hand motions or just call out clues to help. Thomas was visibly enraged by this. He called out to my dad over the noise of everyone guessing, "What are you doing? That's the other team!"

Thomas then got up in an angry huff and walked out of the game as my dad shouted to him down the hall, "It's just a game. We play to have fun!" It was the worst conflict I had seen in my house in a long time! I was so completely embarrassed by Thomas. I thought my dad would never let me marry this guy, but did I even want to? I chased Thomas out and the fight began.

Thomas

I don't mean to brag, but I was a master of arguments. I could turn anything around on anyone. It was a competition, and I was a winner. Lysandra came in the room where I had retreated.

"Why did you get mad at my dad over a game of Taboo?"

I replied with fervor, "It's a game. It's about winning. If you're not playing to win, why are you even playing?"

"To have fun," she said confused.

I told her, "When one team helps the opposing team it ruins the game for everyone and there's no point playing. I'm not going to play games with your family if it's going to be like this."

75

"Please, just while you're here, play to have fun not to win," she pleaded.

I wasn't giving in to her big beautiful blue puppy-dog eyes. I said firmly, "No way. I play to win. You should too. It's not fun to play games with you unless you're trying to win. Don't you want us to be able to have fun together? Don't you want me to have fun? You're ruining games for me!"

I did it! I could see that I broke her; I won. She replied, "I'm sorry. You can play to win. Please come back and play with us? Just promise not to get mad at my dad if he helps the other team; my dad definitely won't change!"

I agreed to come play my hardest and not to say anything to her dad for how he played the game. Lysandra said sorry again and agreed to play her hardest.

Another dragon slain! Cue up Queen's song, "Another One Bites the Dust." I was the triumphant warrior.

Dragons are Everywhere

And no, we aren't talking about your mother-in-law.

When you got married you probably didn't know that there would be so many areas in which you and your spouse could fight. Even if you took multiple pre-marital courses like we did, you were most likely surprised at the number of things about which you would disagree and over which you could fight. Dragons are everywhere!

In the first year of marriage, right after the honeymoon, you start to see these dragons pop up all over the place. Each one is a surprise. She didn't know until they both said I do and moved in together that he was going to play three hours of video games each night. That was a disappointing surprise and a dragon she could slay.

He didn't know until they shared a room that she was going to call her mom and talk every day instead of cuddle with him. That was a sad new reality and a dragon he could slay.

You could fight about the socks he throws on the floor, the check engine light she never tells you about, the way he smells, the way she is late to leave the house, the way he chews his food, or the way she cracks her knuckles. Dragons are everywhere.

The opportunity to fight is all around you. You must choose your battles. Some dragons are worth slaying, but not all must be conquered.

When you look for dragons to slay, you transform your marriage into a tumultuous battlefield and destroy your fairy tale. Every day becomes a fight to win, and both spouses are geared up for constant battle. Both parties are on the defensive when there is any sign of attack. King Solomon warns us how miserable this kind of life is in Proverbs 17:1 when he wrote, *"Better is a dry morsel with quiet than a house full of feasting with strife."* And yet this is exactly the life that so many marriages live in.

A Conquest Seeker

Some people just love to fight. They'll fight over everything and with anyone. You know the kind; they'll argue with a brick wall. They not only fight every battle but are like heat-seeking missiles actively looking for and even creating battles to win. They are seeking dragons to slay and in a marriage relationship, dragons are everywhere.

A person seeking conquests is not fighting for reconciliation; they are fighting to win. This is a person who is chasing their own happiness, setting expectations high and, in the process, destroying everyone's fairy tale. This conquest seeker is toxic. Are you seeking conquest?

Qualities of a person who is seeking conquest:
- Pays attention to every detail
- Looks for ways to criticize
- Loves to win at all costs

- Won't let anything go
- Is happier fighting
- Loves drama
- Corrects every issue
- Sets unreasonably high expectations
- Believes they're always right
- Hates saying sorry
- Is angry
- Complains often
- Overly critical
- Makes up excuses when clearly wrong

Do any of these qualities sound familiar to you? Are you seeking conquest? Are you destroying your fairy tale by trying to slay every dragon? King Solomon continues to write about those who loved to fight, and he likens them to fuel for a fire. Look what he says in Proverbs 26:21: "*As charcoal to hot embers and wood to fire, so is a quarrelsome man for kindling strife.*" When you live to fight, you are the fuel to the fire that will burn up your fairy tale.

Win at All Costs

A conquest seeker will win at all costs. They aren't afraid of low blows. They don't fight fair; they fight to win. This is a person who isn't afraid of going too far in a fight. If they know you have a trigger or know how to hurt you so that you will give up, they will pull that trigger. They fight dirty. They'll hit you below the belt. They will even bite off a chunk of your ear if that's what

it takes. Seriously, Mike, what were you thinking?

No one can hurt us like a spouse can hurt us. When we get married, we begin this beautifully intimate relationship where we open up, tell all our secrets, and become completely vulnerable.

It makes marriage so sweet, but so dangerous. Our spouse has top-secret insider information which can be used for good or for evil.

The information we have about our spouse can break them to pieces. We can destroy their spirit with one sentence, sometimes one single word can do the trick. In Proverbs 18:21 King Solomon makes it very clear just how powerful our words are: *"Death and life are in the power of the tongue, and those who love it will eat its fruits."*

You have a dangerous amount of power over your spouse because of how close you are to them. This is a power that must be used wisely. As we learned from Uncle Ben, "With great power comes great responsibility."

Thomas

During one of our fights about my leaving Lysandra at home with the girls again while I went to watch MMA at Buffalo Wild Wings with my friends, it looked like Lysandra was winning. She was clearly right, and I could see the end of the battle was nearing. I couldn't accept defeat. I had to make the next blow a powerful one.

This was one of those fights that moved throughout the house. Those are the serious ones where you follow the other person in and out of rooms, stalking your prey like a tiger in the night. Somehow, we ended up on the stairs. I looked at my wife, who was sitting several stairs above where I was standing, and strategically took the kill shot.

I said, "You're just like Stephanie, you make it so I don't even want to come home from work."

Lysandra always tried to be nice, kind, and well liked. Stephanie wasn't a nice person, so I knew it would slice up Lysandra's spirit. I also knew how hard Lysandra worked at creating a nice, calm, peaceful home environment for me. She was cleaning constantly, cooking meals exactly to my taste, and making sure that I always had exactly what I needed. She would even ask periodically if there was anything that she could do to make our home better for me. I knew if I attacked our home, she would retreat. I knew how to break her.

I knew how to hurt her more deeply than anyone else. I took my top-secret insider information, and I turned it into a weapon of mass destruction. It worked like a charm. She was devastated. Her entire countenance changed. It was like I watched the air deflate right out of her. I left and went to watch the fights.

Lysandra

Yeah, that one hurt. In fact, the end of that fight holds the title for the worst thing Thomas has ever said to me in twenty years of marriage.

Don't feel too sorry for me, I fight dirty sometimes too. My weapon of choice is not so much mean words but withholding affection. When I get hurt, don't like something Thomas says, or don't get my way, I am cold as ice.

This is fighting dirty for anyone, but it's particularly low for me because I know that Thomas's main love language is physical touch. He feels loved when I hold his hand, allow our legs to touch, rub his head, caress his arm, or cuddle. I can use this weapon tactically and demolish him.

This is my top-secret insider information. This is a weapon only I possess. No one else in the world has the power to hurt Thomas more than I do.

I remember one dragon I was determined to slay was when Thomas embarrassed me in front of a group of people by complaining about his turkey sandwich having mayo on it when he requested no mayo.

It's absolutely astonishing how many of our fights are over

condiments. Sauces are incredibly important in our home! The Osterkamps don't play when it comes to ranch, taco sauce, and mayo.

I was embarrassed that day and was resolute in my determination to win this battle. The plan was to get him to apologize and say I was right. He would regret the day he flipped out over mayo, and I would be the one to bring him to his knees!

I cut off all physical touch immediately. He tried to hold my hand; I crossed my arms. He tried to sit close to me; I scooted away. He tried to put his arm around me; I stood up.

My tactics worked. He did eventually apologize, and I rewarded him with a hug. I'm not proud of this behavior; it's manipulative and fighting dirty.

I can usually strike Thomas with some swift uppercuts by withholding physical touch. This is my strategy when fighting to win rather than fighting for resolution. This is how I destroy our fairy tale.

Don't Be a Fool

You are a fool to fight every battle. You make yourself a fool if you're always fighting your spouse to win. You don't care about resolution; you just want to win. You've turned what's supposed to be the most loving, peaceful relationship into a quarreling combat zone. It's like that meme that says, "We never go to bed angry; we've been up for three days." What a foolish way to live. King Solomon certainly thought so when he wrote, "*It is an honor for a man to keep aloof from strife, but every fool will be quarreling*" (Proverbs 20:3).

It is foolish to fight against your spouse when they are your teammate. You are unhealthy. Craig and Amy Groeschel say it so precisely in their book *From This Day Forward*.

Here's the reality: all couples fight. Why? Well, the short answer is because we're all sinners, and our sinfulness leads us to do selfish things. It's inevitable, unavoidable, and inherent in any relationship where true intimacy occurs. All couples fight, but healthy couples fight fair. Unhealthy couples fight dirty, with below the belt jabs, succor punches, angry accusations, and bitter grudges. Healthy couples fight for resolution. Unhealthy couples fight for personal victory.[8]

You're on the same team yet, when you fight, you position yourself in opposition to your most valuable player. Stop viewing your marriage as a battlefield where you're on one side of the line and your spouse is on the other. When you do this, Jesus says that you are setting up your fairy tale to crumble down around you. He states in Mark 3:25, "*And if a house is divided against itself, that house will not be able to stand.*"

If you continue to fight against your spouse to win rather than resolve, you are a fool, and your marriage cannot stand. You are destroying your fairy tale.

6

Leave the Sword in the Stone

Choosing Your Battles

Once upon a time . . . there was a boy who put the sword back in the stone and became a peaceful knight.

Thomas

I still have the ability to destroy, conquer, and dominate. I have that killer instinct. I am a fighter; I am a winner. I can break Lysandra's spirit with a single sentence. I choose not to be the conquering warrior anymore. I choose to be a peaceful knight and it's creating our fairy tale.

Lysandra

I'm not a fighter. I have no desire to pursue battles unless there's a significant injustice. I have learned that I am conflict averse.

Any hint of a person who may be upset or unhappy with another person makes me immediately uncomfortable, even if it isn't about me. I get this feeling throughout my body when there's conflict. It's an incredibly strong wave I can feel physically. The wave starts at my heart and crashes out in all directions covering my body in a tight, hot, physical discomfort. I become aware of my blood pumping rapidly and I can feel a headache form from the tightness in my chest creeping up my neck into my skull. It's so terrible.

This is a big reason I will do anything to keep the peace. Including saying sorry for everything. I just want the fighting to end even if it means I'm the perpetual loser. It sounds like I'm the noble martyr, but there's nothing noble about taking every hit at the cost of the truth. When I lie and say "I'm fine" when I'm not, this is anything but honorable. This is still unhealthy and dishonest. It is lying to pretend everything is okay. It's deceptive to act like I'm sorry when I know I'm not to blame.

Thomas

When you pair Lysandra's aversion to conflict with my love of winning and selfishness, it made for a rough marriage, at least for one of us. I viewed every fight as an opportunity to win, so I went after every battle. Fought every fight. Slayed every dragon. I thought everything was going great. I thought we were happy. I was wrong.

There was a big fight driving home from church one night, neither of us can remember what it was over, but it felt big at the time. I, in my usual conquering spirit, had Lysandra apologizing again through tears. I was just calming down, you know, the way you do after returning home a conquering hero from the battlefield, when she looked at me sadly. She said in a quiet, broken, and defeated voice, "I don't understand how I'm always the one who is wrong. I am the only one who says sorry. I must be a terrible person."

Something changed in me that day. I realized in that moment that my winning had broken my best friend who I love more than anything and anyone in the entire world. I felt very small.

I did it—I said those two words which were never spoken in my childhood home. I said genuinely for the first time, "I'm sorry."

Lysandra and I were never as close as that moment. For the first time we had reconciliation. It showed me that resolution was actually better than winning in a marriage relationship. I learned the way to be a winner in marriage is to seek resolution, not dominion. I began pursuing peace and resolution rather than total domination.

I'm a changed man. Now I say sorry when I think something I said may have been taken wrong. I'll apologize when my heart is smitten over something even when no one has told me I've wronged them. I can honestly say this way of living feels more like winning.

Choose Your Battles

Not all battles need to be fought, but some do. Use wisdom in choosing your battels. Ask God to show you when to fight and when to let it go.

Some things can be ignored. When your wife uses a tone you don't feel is respectful, you don't necessarily need to gear up for battle. You may want to consider what she is going through, think about if the tone is actually about you or just because she's stressed, and decide if this is worth the cost of pursuing. Is this a dragon that needs to be slain, or can you leave the sword in the stone?

If your husband stays late at work again without texting you, you don't necessarily have to get out your sword and prepare to slice and dice. You may want to pause and remember his work is a way to provide for your family, he probably meant to text but forgot, and choose not to slay this particular dragon this time.

When choosing to fight or not, ask yourself these few helpful questions:
- Is this anger about me?
- Is this something I can overlook?
- Is my spouse overly stressed right now?
- Is this an oversight or intentional?
- Is this a reoccurring offense or an isolated incident?
- Is this an opportunity for grace?

Sometimes battles don't need to be fought because your spouse isn't intentionally doing that to hurt you, they are having other stresses in their life that seem to be spilling out into your relationship, or it isn't really that big of a deal in the grand scheme of things.

The Apostle Paul gave one of the greatest definitions of love ever recorded in 1 Corinthians 13. This is the chapter on love that is often read at weddings to celebrate the love that the couple has for each other. Notice what he wrote in verse 5 about letting some things go: *"Love suffers long and is not easily provoked."* Paul knew that not everything was worth fighting for.

Here are a few examples of battles not worth fighting:
- Your spouse is short with you.
- Your spouse forgets something they said they would do.
- This is an isolated incident of thoughtlessness.
- This is a simple difference of opinion.

- Your spouse is actively trying to change their negative behavior.
- What they're doing is not wrong, but annoying.
- You and your spouse disagree on a trivial matter.

Here are a few examples of battles worth fighting:
- Your spouse is unfaithful.
- You are being personally attacked.
- You are protecting your children.
- This is repeated inconsideration of your feelings.
- You are being asked to disobey God.

Fighting For Resolution

Some dragons need to be slain. Some fights are worth fighting. When there is a battle worth choosing, you need to remember that your spouse is not the enemy, they are your teammate. You have to change your mindset from fighting to win, to fighting for resolution. In doing so, you will cease to destroy your fairy tale and begin to create it.

When fighting for resolution, follow these rules to fight fair:
1. Pick the time of your fight with careful consideration.

   If your spouse just walked in the door after a long, hard day's work, this is not the time to begin a fight. If you were up all night with the baby and are sleepless and exhausted, do not begin a fight. If there are other people around, including your children, don't start your fight. If your spouse is too emotional to interact, don't bring up the problem and argue. If you are raging with anger, don't start a discussion.

   Only fight when both spouses are well rested, emotionally ready, and alone. Begin by saying something positive and loving, then bring up the issue at hand in a controlled, calm tone.

2. Take a break.

   If you're in the middle of a fight and you get so worked up that you can no longer stick to the rules, take a break. Go to separate spaces, take a walk, or sit in silence and just breathe. Be sure to restart the argument in a reasonable amount of time so that you don't have a bunch of unresolved arguments hanging over your heads.

3. Never say *never*.

   You should never say *never* when fighting and always refrain from saying *always*. Using words like never and always only escalates the fight. They are also untrue.

   If you say your spouse always leaves his socks on the floor, the only way that's true is if he never one time picked up his socks. So, it's probably not true. So don't say never. If you say your spouse is always late, that's not true unless she has never once been on time. Most likely that's not true, so don't say always.

   These words immediately put your spouse into a defensive posture and move you both further from resolution. Saying always will always hinder reconciliation and saying never will never bring unity to your relationship.

4. Don't hit below the belt.

Hitting below the belt is using that top-secret insider information against your spouse. If your spouse has deep insecurities about their body and you call them ugly and fat, you are fighting dirty. If your spouse is insecure about his ability to provide for the family, and you say you can't afford anything nice because he doesn't make enough money, you are fighting dirty.

Don't say things you'll regret later. Don't create new things for which you will need to apologize for later. Hitting below the belt includes name-calling, swearing, insulting, and all personal attacks. These are all off limits in a fair fight.

5. Listen to understand, not to respond.

    When in the middle of a fight, listen. Get rid of distractions. Turn off the TV, put down the phone, and give your spouse your full attention. Listen to understand rather than using their speaking time to prepare your strategic rebuttal. This is the one you vowed to love and honor forever, listen to what they're saying. Try to understand exactly what they mean.

6. Remember there are two sides.

    When you feel passionate about an issue, it's difficult to see anything but your own side of the matter. Attempt to see things from their perspective. Their perspective is as real to them as yours is to you. The way they feel is just as valid as the way you feel. Value their feelings. Seek to understand their point of view the way you want them to seek to understand yours. Remember there's always a possibility you're wrong. Yes, even YOU can be wrong.

7. Don't yell.

    Yelling never helps anyone. Speak in a cool, calm tone. Speak with respect and love in your voice. If they feel like you're yelling, you're yelling. Even the most intelligent argument sounds like an attack if it's yelled. Smooth your tone. Relax. Go back to rule two if you can't refrain from yelling right now.

8. Don't deal in extremes.

    Don't take everything they say to the most ridiculous extreme, so they no longer have a point. This is unfair to your spouse. If they say, "I wish you had more time for me and the kids." Don't respond with, "Well then, I guess I'll just quit my job so I can stay home and cuddle with you and play with the kids. Then we'll lose the house and end up living in a cardboard box, but at least we'll be together. Is that what you want?" This is extreme arguing, and it never gets you anywhere.

9. Don't bring up the past.

    Keep it current. Only fight one fight at a time. When you're in the middle of an argument, don't begin to bring up anything they ever did in the past to hurt you. Talk about the current offense. If this is a reoccurring offense, discussing the many times this same wrongdoing has been committed is appropriate. The reoccurring behavior should be addressed. If there are other unrelated hurts left unresolved from the past, set them aside and bring them up at another appropriate time. See rule one.

10. Don't use the "D" word.

Never threaten to divorce your spouse. The "D" word should be completely off limits in your fights. Threatening to abandon the other to get your way or win a fight is a low blow. It's manipulation and totally unacceptable in a fair fight. Remember, the goal is restoration, and threatening divorce is the exact opposite of resolution.

Lysandra

Thomas and I fight, and we think you should too. We also plan to continue to fight in the future. Fighting is good. It clears the air, allows each partner to express themselves, gives opportunity to apologize, offer forgiveness, and can lead to some great make-up sex. More than that, when done correctly it deepens your relationship in an inexplicable way.

Thomas

I want to interject something for all the husbands right here since Lysandra brought up make-up sex. Guys, don't start fights just so you can get make-up sex. It doesn't work, and believe me I have tried, a lot.

Lysandra

No, it doesn't work. We can see right through that little scheme, but I will tell you that you will get a lot further by being loving and affectionate. Can we get back on topic now?

One of our most recent fights was a great example of how to fight fair. I had been working so hard for such a long time without enough rest, and it finally caught up with me. I took the girls on a Monday morning to homeschool Co-op until one o'clock in the afternoon, then went straight from Co-op to the DMV to wait in a long line for what felt like hours. By the time we got home, it was nearing three o'clock and we were all so hungry! We immediately made a quick lunch of chicken and steamed broccoli in a bag! We dished up the food equally, thanked the Lord, and began to eat.

It was just then that Thomas walked into the kitchen and said in utter contempt, "What! There's nothing left for me? Nice! I guess I'll just have a cold can of tuna." I immediately offered him my food, saying I didn't care what I had to eat. He could eat this hot food. To which he declined quickly and walked up the stairs eating his tuna straight out of the can. I felt so guilty that I hadn't thought of him; that didn't last long.

Crushing guilt turned rather quickly into outraged anger. I started to think, "I work outside the home, I am homeschooling *his* children, I'm running this house, I'm taking care of the van, I'm going to Co-op, I'm going to the DMV, and much much more. Why isn't he making *me* lunch? I should've walked into the house to a nice hot lunch myself, but now I'm being made to feel guilty that I didn't think of him. I just assumed that he already ate since he had been home all day and it was now 3:00 p.m.!" I was absolutely livid!

I knew he had men's leadership group later that night, during which I had spiritual mentoring. I knew that this was not the right time to talk about it, so I kept quiet and went about my day. After his leadership group and my mentoring were over, I asked him to go for a walk.

It was already dark, and the neighborhood was quiet. This wasn't a problem for us, because we've learned when we fight, we fight fair, which means no yelling allowed! We held hands and quietly fought as we walked through the neighborhood in the night. I expressed why my guilt turned into anger in a calm way after telling Thomas how much I loved him. He listened to me rant and vent quietly, and then came back with, "I had no idea you felt this way; I thought everything was fine! I'll try to help more. But you're going to have to tell me when you need help." We both agreed, hugged it out, and then went home to enjoy a closer relationship than we had before.

After twenty years of marriage, Thomas and I almost always fight fair. I'm pleased to say that we haven't had an unfair fight in many sweet years. It's created a lovely fairy tale in which to live.

Thomas

The way I fight now compared to how I grew up and how I used to fight at the beginning of our marriage are as different as night and day. We fight so respectfully and maturely you almost can't classify our fights as fights; they're more like serious discussions.

One of our fair fights that took place years ago, when we had just learned the value of a fair fight, was in our church with other people nearby. We were working yet again on this hundred-plus-year-old building. This time we had the help of another couple in our church, who were also our very close friends.

We were on the third flight of stairs where we were working to paint, change light fixtures, and deep clean. It was a lot of work, and we were tired. I kept telling Lysandra she needed to go back over her paint job. She had missed spots even after two coats were applied. I helpfully said, "There's another one over here. You missed a whole area over here. By the ceiling over there there's a bad spot."

She was frantically following my instructions running around with her paint brush. As time went on, she began to become frustrated. In the past she would have simply swallowed her anger and kept painting. Later that anger would mellow out and settle in her heart as resentment.

Things were different now. We had been married for thirteen years and had significantly grown. Lysandra was no longer the perpetual loser. She understood how to speak the truth of her feelings and fight for resolution.

She gave me *the eyes*. They said, *Follow me into the office please*. I followed her through the door; she shut it. We began a calm, controlled whisper fight. We sat on the floor close to one another, our knees touching. Lysandra explained that she felt I was being too picky, and when I only pointed out the failures in her work without saying something positive, it made her feel like all her work was insufficient and unappreciated.

In the past I would have pulled the sword out of the stone and began to demolish my wife. I would have said something like, "You're being too sensitive. I'm trying to help you. Just accept my critiques as helpful and fix your mistakes."

In the earlier years I would have had her apologizing to me for not accepting my help and being overly sensitive. Now I don't want to win; I want my relationship to flourish.

What I said *instead* reflected the growth and maturity that had come from failing so many times in the past. I whispered, "I'm sorry. I understand why you feel this way. I'll do better about pointing out positive things as well as helping you catch the bare spots. You have worked so hard, and you did a great job. I do appreciate you."

We hugged and walked out of the office and returned to working with our friends. There was no blow up, there was no name-calling or yelling, there was no hidden resentment. Everyone was honest. It was a simple discussion for resolution.

Fighting Can Be a Beautiful Thing

Seeking to never fight is unrealistic. Trying to never disagree is unattainable. Attempting to never argue is unreasonable. Fighting fair is a beautiful thing in marriage. It's a way of seeking God rather than seeking your own happiness. Discussing issues in a kind, loving way is a great reflection of our relationship with Jesus.

Choose to fight only necessary battles. Fight over only the essentials. When you do fight, fight right. If you can learn to fight fair, you will create a lovely fairy tale.

7

Kissing Your Frog

Trying to Change Your Spouse

Once upon a time . . . there was a girl who couldn't stop kissing her frog, desperately hoping for a prince to appear in its place.

Lysandra

"Why won't he be nice to me? He says he loves me. Why is he so mean? I hate him!"

I couldn't believe it. I couldn't believe I was thinking thoughts like this about my Thomas. I simultaneously loved and hated him. It was very confusing.

I was so completely convinced that I would never think "I hate my husband" before we got married. I thought I would never be that kind of wife or that kind of person.

I read a helpful book before I got married. We were engaged and I went to a Bible study on marriage; we read the book *The Excellent Wife* by Martha Peace. I read in the book that a wife could be so mad at her husband she could think, *"I hate him!"*[9]

I was appalled by this disgraceful thought. My reaction was arrogant: "No way! Never! I'll never think, 'I hate Thomas.' I love him too much, and I've never hated anyone my whole life." Marriage can change even the nicest little Iowa girl into a person who hates!

So, there I was after one of our "Thomas must win, Lysandra must lose fights" thinking, "I hate him! He's so mean to me." I almost feel like I can now empathize with how the apostle Peter felt when he heard the rooster crow after denying Jesus for the third time. I said I'd never do that or think that, then the words of that book came back to me in a dark moment of shame as well as the remembrance of my judgmental thoughts toward the wife who could hate her husband.

Guilt crashed over me like an ocean wave. I've never hated anyone, not ever. Who have I become? Not to mention, I love this jerk more than anything. Was this the beginning of us getting divorced? I'm a zero to sixty kind of person and tend to emotionally panic rather quickly.

Then I realized, I knew of a book where I read about what to do when you hate your husband. I went back to the book. Martha wrote words that helped me get through this period in our marriage, and I often referred to the book in times of seeming hopelessness in my marriage, but we'll save that for the next chapter.

I'm sorry to say hating my husband wasn't an isolated incident. There were other times I hated my Thomas and wanted desperately to change him. I remember sitting and strategizing what I could do to potentially change him. Maybe if I say this or that. If I cry, he'll see how much he's hurting me, then he'll feel guilty and change. If I make yet another appeal to him, he'll understand and change.

I couldn't stop kissing my frog. I kept dreaming that one day he would turn into the prince I wanted him to be.

Thomas

I never knew my wife had moments when she hated me. To be honest, even if I had, I'm pretty sure I wouldn't have changed anything. I was stuck in a rut of winning, never being wrong, and never saying sorry. I thought I was a great guy, and nothing needed to change.

Lysandra on the other hand needed a couple of tweaks. She was so emotional all the time. Who has unlimited tears like that? I thought at some point she'd dry up, but no. There were always more tears.

She was controlling and obsessive too. There were times when I was drinking my drink and she would come take my cup, wash it, and put it back in the cabinet. I'd be like, "Where is my cup?" She'd say, "I washed it and put it away in the cabinet; I'm cleaning up." Sometimes I felt like I had to chug my drink just so I could finish it. I had to protect my drinks, so they didn't get taken. I assume this is how prisoners feel at mealtimes! I had to pull it in close, get my elbows high, and dare her to come and try to take it this time.

My plan for changing Lysandra was much less strategic and more off-the-cuff direct. Truthfully, I had no plan at all. I'd say things like, "Chill out, sit down, I'm still drinking!" when she was cleaning obsessively. Or when she was crying yet again, I'd simply say what I thought: "It's not that big of a deal, relax."

Needless to say, changing her didn't go well. I was kissing my frog time and again only to open my eyes and see the same frog every time. Where was the princess that I thought I married?

Frog-like Behaviors

There are many character traits we may be tempted to

change in our spouse. The list of potential annoyances is endless. Some areas you wish you could change about your spouse seem simple, yet they cause these almost visceral responses from us. When months turn into years, annoyances become grievances that eventually become disdain. The surprising thing is that the very habit or behavior you thought was so cute before you got married can end up being the most repulsive trait after a few years. Maybe you feel like you married your prince and then after the wedding they turned into a frog.

Here are a few frog-like behaviors we found women will most likely desire to change about their spouse:
- Be more attentive to my needs.
- Listen to me.
- Be a spiritual leader.
- Be nice to me.
- Show me love.
- Be interested in me.
- Take time for me.
- Help with the kids.
- Help me around the house.
- Plan dates.
- Give me presents.
- Work harder.

Here are a few frog-like behaviors we found men will most likely desire to change about their spouse:
- Be a happier wife.
- Be interested in and enjoy sex.
- Have more fun.
- Spend time with me.
- Don't criticize.
- Be interested in my interests.

- Stop nagging.

How Men Kiss Their Frog

In our experience in dealing with couples and in our own marriage, we see that men typically approach changing their spouse differently than women do. Men tend to be more direct. A husband will usually tell his wife what he wishes she would change right to her face.

This sounds good, right? Direct, honest, and open—all good habits in marriage, right? Well, yes, done in the right way in the right timing with the right motives, which isn't always the case. Often as a man seeks to change his wife, he decides to do it during a fight in an explosion of anger.

When a man has had enough of whatever annoying behavior, he will snap and begin to yell about the trait he hates about his wife. It may come out accompanied with insults and escalation words like "never" and "always."

We find that with men, there is very little planning or prep work in changing their spouse. It's more of a "you pushed me over the edge of a cliff, I'm done with this, knock it off" kind of outburst.

How Women Kiss Their Frog

Women tend to be much different when they go about changing their spouse. A woman usually has a plan. These plans can range from a loose idea of what she wants to do to a thirty-seven-point plan of attack.

We find women will see the area they are frustrated with and think things through. As they see what they dislike about their husband, they will begin their tactical development. Each approach may be different, but typically there is a plan.

The plan may be a way to appeal to her husband's emotions and thereby produce the change. In this case she may try crying to make him feel bad for her and thus change his behavior. She may try withholding affection to allure him into shaping up. She may berate him with her words, attempting to break his spirit, generating the change she desires.

The woman's plan may be to appeal to his mind. This can be just as manipulative. She may bring her case to him, arguing her point and seeking the desired verdict: his choosing to change. If desperate enough she will say anything in the debate to win the case. She may use criticism or sarcasm as her plan of attack, making him second guess his decisions and behavior.

She may convince herself that she is blameless because she only implied something but didn't actually say it. She may think, "I didn't actually say anything wrong; I just implied it so I'm guilt-free." It becomes easier and easier to deceive yourself into believing your sarcasm and mini jabs are innocent.

Lysandra

I remember thinking, "What can I do to make him change?" I remember thinking through different scenarios and projecting the effectiveness of saying and doing different things.

One time I attacked Thomas's emotional defenses to try to get him to apologize and be nice to me. We had a nasty fight. He dug his heels in. He refused to apologize for the thing I felt was his fault. I was so angry, and I wanted to hit him where it hurts so he would break.

I took my pillow and blanket and left the room that night. I know what you're thinking: "Isn't the wife supposed to make the husband sleep on the couch?" I was smart enough to know there was absolutely no way on earth I was going to get Thomas to leave our room and sleep on the couch. So, I left.

I was lying there in the living room stewing over my big loss and hoping this Hail Mary would change my husband. I was sure he would come apologetically crawling out to my side, beg for forgiveness, and change his behavior. I knew I was attacking him where he was vulnerable because Thomas loves to cuddle; he hates to sleep without me.

Sure enough, about ten minutes later, I heard the bedroom door open. I thought, "Aha, here he comes a changed, repentant man." He rounded the corner, and with a firm resolve in his voice he said, "Lysandra, get up, you're not sleeping on the couch. Get to bed, now."

My planning, my attack, my strategy was an epic failure. He hadn't had an epiphany or a change. He was just angrier now, and somehow the tables had turned, and I was in the wrong for walking away in the middle of an unresolved argument.

Before we got married, we promised one another we would always sleep together. We promised we would never leave the room. Both of us gave our word that we wouldn't do the thing I had just done. I broke my promise, and it didn't even work to change him.

Thomas

One way, unbeknownst to me, I tried to change Lysandra was by trying to change her extroverted tendency. I already shared with you how much I wanted her all to myself, especially when we first got married. After being with people and working all day, I didn't want to go places or do anything, and I especially didn't want to see people all the time.

It felt like we worked constantly, and being a pastor, I was always with people and going to events. Spending time with people and going places felt like more work to me; it totally drained my batteries. I married a super extrovert. Lysandra charges her batteries by being around people; the bigger the group the better for her.

I hated this insatiable desire she had to always go and do and be with people. I immediately tried to change this about my wife, rather than compromising with her. I would just say "No." I would tell her, "I'm not going, and neither are you. We're staying home."

She would be sad but would agree to stay home. I didn't realize that I was trying to change who she was. She needed to go and do and be with people. I was subconsciously trying to change her into an introvert like me. It didn't occur to me till much later that I could let her go without me and when she got home, she would be happier, more fulfilled, and we would have a better time when we were together because of it.

The Motive behind Frog Kissing

There may be a few pure motives to changing your spouse, but most of the reasons we kiss our frog repeatedly is because we want our life to be better. Chasing our own happiness is the true motive of changing our spouse.

Pure motives are a possible reason for trying to change your spouse, such as wanting them to have a deeper relationship with their Heavenly Father or the desire for them to have a better relationship with their children.

Most likely your motives for trying to change your spouse are selfish. They may be trying to camouflage themselves within pure motives, but they are selfish at their heart. For instance, it seems noble to want to help your spouse be a better employee by nagging them to get up earlier and get to work on time. The hidden motive under that noble motive is that you don't want to change your spending habits if your spouse were to lose their job.

It appears your motives are pure when you want to change your spouse into being more interested in sex. It's biblical to have a sexual relationship with your spouse, it's good for them, and it will make the two of you closer. The motives that are camouflaged behind those pure motives are a desire for self-fulfillment, despite how your spouse feels and what they're going through.

It seems reasonable to try to change your spouse into a better help around the house. If they help you, you will have more time to spend with them. The house will be a more pleasant home for them. You will be happier which benefits them too. The true motives hiding out behind these motives are that you're tired and want more help. You don't want to do it all by yourself. You feel used.

It sounds like a good motive to change your spouse to help them be healthier. They will then live a longer life with good health and a better quality of life. The true motives sneaking around your heart may be that you were more attracted to them when they were a certain size or had a certain physique that pleased your selfish desires. Maybe you miss the big muscles or the tiny waste.

The bottom line is this: Most of the time, we want to change our spouse into someone who is more pleasing to us personally. We want them to look, act, talk, and do what appeals to us, which is self-centered and does not honor God.

Have you ever listened to someone try to convince you that they were trying to help you when you knew at the heart of it, they just wanted to sell you something which would benefit them? That's what it's like when we try to convince God that we have pure motives to change our spouse, but the real reason is our own happiness, convenience, or self-serving desires.

Your Spouse Has Weaknesses

If you married another human being, you married a person with weaknesses. Your spouse has faults, addictions, character flaws, annoying behaviors, and bad habits. They get on your nerves and fail you. They make mistakes and disappoint you. They are human just like you are.

As you identify and notice your spouse's weaknesses, you

may wish they were more like someone else's husband or wife. You may start seeing other marriages and deceive yourself into thinking they have no problems or weaknesses. That is not the case. Every marriage has problems, challenges, and issues. Every spouse has weaknesses, character flaws, and bad habits.

If you think the grass is greener, it may be fake.

Don't be fooled into thinking life would be better with someone else or if your spouse was more like someone else. That isn't true; it's a deception. Your spouse is who they are supposed to be. We all have room to grow, and we all have things that we need to work on, but it isn't the job of a spouse to change those things. It is the job of the Holy Spirit. Our responsibility is to love and accept them.

You are commanded to love them despite their issues. For some reason this is so difficult for us to understand even though we want them to love us despite our issues. We must give them the same acceptance we expect from them.

The Apostle Paul wrote about this in Romans 15:7: "Therefore *welcome one another as Christ has welcomed you, for the glory of God.*" It's not your job to change your spouse but to accept them for who they are and who they are not. We are to love them with an unconditional Jesus-like love. Look what He taught in John 13:34: "*A new commandment I give to you, that you love one another: just as I have loved you, you also are to love one another.*"

Trying to change your spouse is refusing to accept them as God designed them. When you work to change your spouse, you will create frustration for yourself and for your spouse. You take away the opportunity for them to be the real person they were designed to be. You replace the peace and the comfort of being their authentic self with the heavy weight of being a fake version of themself who is working hard to earn love and acceptance.

Trying to change your spouse will destroy your fairy tale.

8

Love Your Frog

Accepting Your Spouse as They Are

Once upon a time . . . there was a girl who chose to love her frog just the way he was.

Lysandra

Thomas isn't a frog, not really, but sometimes I felt he was. As I shared earlier there were even a couple times I thought those dreadful words, "I hate him!" The first time was when I was pregnant with our second daughter; I was feeling unloved and unappreciated. I don't like to give excuses for women's behavior, and I hate it when women blame their monthly cycle for why they act a certain way. I have to admit though, the worst years of our marriage were the seven years I was pregnant and nursing. I look back and realize my hormones were all over the place. I felt things deeper, got hurt easier, was always exhausted, and was much more irritable.

So, there I was, six months pregnant, holding my one-year-old, begging my husband not to leave me and go out with friends. He left. I thought, "I hate him!" The funny thing is, I didn't hate him at all. I loved him so much and wanted him to be with me, but I was angry.

"I'm a terrible person to have a thought like this. Who have I become?"

That was the moment I realized, I read in that book before I got married that this thought might come into the mind of a wife. I never thought it would happen to me, but it did. I went back to the book *The Excellent Wife*. Martha Peace wrote words that helped me get through this period in our marriage, and I often referred to the book in times of seeming hopelessness in my marriage.

She referenced replacement theology—when we replace false thoughts with true thoughts. Replace, *"I hate him!"* with *"I don't feel love for him right now, but I choose to love him by responding in a kind way."*[10]

Later in a portion on bitterness, she explained the difference between bitter thoughts—*"I hate him"*—and kind, tenderhearted, and forgiving thoughts—*"I can show love to him whether I feel like it or not. 1 Corinthians 13:1-7"*[11]

I did exactly what the book said. I replaced my thoughts. I thought purposefully, "I don't feel love for my husband right now, but I choose to be kind to him." I showed love to him when I didn't feel like it. Doing this genuinely and consistently drew my husband's heart closer to me. His love for me grew and grew over the years.

That really helped me get through those early years. Eventually, I got to the place where I was happy for my husband to go out with his friends. I got to the point where I didn't like everything about Thomas, but I accepted him for who he was, the positive and negative qualities.

I stopped kissing my frog attempting to change him into an unrealistic prince and accepted him as he was. My life got better when I did that. I was more relaxed; I could enjoy my life. As it turns out, working to change someone is exhausting and frustrating.

Thomas

I began to accept Lysandra's extroverted ways when I began to understand them better. Once I understood she needed people to recharge her battery, I would suggest she go to family events without me. When she felt like it was important for me to attend certain things, I would show up happily to support my wife. I would allow her to have people over more often. Sometimes I would hide in my room, and sometimes I would work harder at interacting with people for my Love.

When I stopped trying to make her become an introvert like me, she was happier. When she was happier, I was happier. Life is better when you stop trying to change your spouse.

Every Prince Has Frog-like Qualities

Unfortunately, it seems like the only two options depicted in our fairy tales are a perfect, handsome prince or an ugly, horrible frog. The reality is no one is all frog or all prince. We all have prince-like qualities just as we all have frog-like qualities.

No person is all bad or all good in a marriage relationship. We have all been created by a loving God. This loving God also gifted each of us with talents and abilities. Yes, even your frog has prince-like qualities. King David reminds us in Psalm 139:13–14, *"For you formed my inward parts; you knitted me together in in my mother's womb. I praise you, for I am fearfully and wonderfully made. Wonderful are your works; my soul knows it very well."*

Just as we are all uniquely created and gifted by God, we're all fallen, sinful human beings with character flaws. Paul tells us in Romans 3:23 that *"all have sinned and fall short of the glory of God."* Every one of us sin; we miss the mark. No one is perfect. You are flawed; your spouse is flawed.

The problem is that so often we want our spouse to recognize our gifts, talents, and positive traits. We expect our partner to overlook our flaws while we are working to change theirs. Jesus called out people for that very thing in Matthew 7:3–5:

> *Why do you see the speck that is in your brother's eye, but do not notice the log that is in your own eye? Or how can you say to your brother, 'Let me take the speck out of your eye,' when there is the log in your own eye? You hypocrite, first take the log out of your own eye, and then you will see clearly to take the speck out of your brother's eye.*

As you look at your spouse and see flaws, bad habits, and unattractive qualities, you may be tempted to try to fix all those negative areas. We must remember to look in the mirror. Understand your own flaws and negative traits and focus on working on those. Remember that we're all a work in progress. You are growing and so is your spouse, but not everyone grows at the same rate. You may retrain your thinking to "I don't like what he does that, but he puts up with me and my flaws."

We must change our thinking. We need to mature enough to accept our spouse just as they are and love them as God made them. We must stop trying to *fix* them.

We are called to love one another thirteen times in the New Testament. Love is a command and is especially applicable to you toward your spouse. You are to love your spouse. Real love is unconditional. Godly love isn't based on what someone looks like, says, does, or doesn't do. True love is an outpouring of the love of God.

God loves you unconditionally. The Apostle Paul reminds us in Romans 5:6–8 that He loved us while we were still His enemy. *"For while we were still weak, at the right time Christ died for the ungodly. For one will scarcely die for a righteous person— though perhaps for a good person one would dare even to die but God shows his love for us in that while we were still sinners, Christ died for us."* If God loves us unconditionally and sacrificially and we are to love like God, then we are to love our spouse unconditionally and sacrificially—whether or not they deserve it. We love them because it is the right thing to do.

True, unconditional love accepts. When you can accept your spouse, including their annoying habits and their frustrating flaws, you will experience the joy of loving someone in a real way. It isn't loving for you to try to change your spouse; it's selfish.

Loving unconditionally doesn't mean overlooking or accepting sin. Sin is always wrong and unacceptable. If your spouse is living in sin without any attempt to correct their behavior, it may be time to get some help. Go to your pastor or a local counselling ministry and get help for your spouse if necessary.

We are also not telling you to stay in an abusive relationship. If your spouse is abusive to you or your children, don't accept that behavior. You are not called to live in an abusive marriage. If this is your situation, you need to get out and get help immediately.

Getting out of abuse doesn't always mean divorce. You can work on your marriage from a safe distance. Before working on repairing your marriage, get to a safe place! Protect yourself and your children by getting to safety. If you are in this type of situation, we recommend the book *Enough is Enough* by David E. Clarke. In this book he explains what an abusive relationship is and a plan to get out and then work on the marriage from a safe place.

Lysandra

It may not be that you hate your spouse and want to change them but are frustrated because you don't understand why they do what they do or why they react the way that they do. When you don't understand why they do what they do, it is easy to think it's an area where they need to change, when there may be a simple explanation.

For our entire relationship, including before marriage, I detested helping Thomas with projects. If he was going to attempt to fix something or build something, it was going to be miserable for me. You could count on him getting mad, throwing things, yelling, or losing his temper.

I dislike any unhappy situation, so this was always uncomfortable for me, and I took it all personally. I thought, "He's mad at me for asking him to fix this. He's angry that I needed his help." These thoughts were a big part of why I began to learn how to repair and build things for myself, so he wouldn't get angry with me.

Last year I began to paint the exterior of our two-story Florida home. We decided to replace the dated outside light fixtures while the rest of the house was getting a face lift. Thomas's job was replacing the light fixtures while I painted. He asked that dreaded question, "Can you come help me?"

I knew it was going to end in him being angry. Sure enough, in about ten minutes, he was repeating his project catch phrase, "Why can't anything be easy!" He could tell I was upset. I was less reserved due to the exhaustion of all the painting.

"What's wrong?" he asked.

I told him I love to help him, but I hate helping him with projects because it always ends with him mad at me.

He explained to me why he gets like this, and it changed me, not him. He said, "It's not about you. I'm just venting."

I can understand venting. If it weren't for Thomas, I would

have given up on most everything in my life. He is my emotional sounding board. I come home to him and let it all out. I express my feelings to him, and he listens patiently and genuinely cares about my cares. I vent to him daily!

Viewing his outbursts during projects as venting has made me understand he doesn't need to change; I need to change. I don't need to take it personally; it's not about me. I need to listen to his frustrations the way he listens to mine. He just needs someone to vent to. I want to be that person for my Thomas.

All these years, I wanted to change him into a quiet, happy person when he did projects, but that was just because I didn't understand why he was behaving the way he was behaving. I now understand why he acts the way he does, and it has helped us so much. I accept him as he is, even during projects. I also learned that since he isn't mad at me for asking for his help with a project, I can ask him to help me with even more projects.

Why Are You the Way You Are?

If there is a behavior you've been trying to change about your spouse, don't just let it go. Seek to understand it. Ask good questions in a loving way.

You may want to say something like, "I love you and I want to understand why you seem so upset that I do this certain thing. Why do you think that is such a trigger for you? I love you, but I don't care for this habit you have." You can ask, "Where did this habit start? Why do you think it's so difficult for you to stop? Are you trying to change this habit, or do you want it to continue to be present in your life?"

Thomas

You will find fault if you're looking for it. I look for the best in Lysandra and that's what I find. I know that she has faults, but I choose not to focus on them.

Lysandra is the hardest working and most driven person that I know. She is multitalented and lives her life multitasking. Most of the time that is a great thing, except when it comes to cooking while at the same time doing a variety of other tasks.

I love my wife's cooking! There are few things in life that I enjoy more than the food that my wife makes for me. She makes everything from lasagna to shepherd's pie, homemade mac and cheese, a variety of soups, and a whole lot more. And don't get me started on the pies, cakes, cookies, and everything else!

There are times that she loses focus on what she is doing in the kitchen because of the other things that she is getting done at the same time, and that leads to the occasional overcooked meal. That used to make me so upset, and I tried to change the way that she is wired to get her to focus on just one thing at a time.

But as I have matured as a husband, and grown to value her for who she is, I choose to focus on all the things that she is accomplishing and not the few mistakes that she makes from time to time. Far too often we do the exact opposite. We focus in on the few mistakes instead of the wealth of good things that our spouses are doing.

What Are You Looking For?

Have you ever noticed that when you get a new vehicle all the sudden you realize everyone everywhere has the same vehicle? It's because once you buy that new car, you're more aware of that car. If it's a red SUV you suddenly notice every red SUV on the road.

If you are looking for flaws in your spouse, you will surely find them. They are there; we're not denying that. However, your spouse's flaws are only as noticeable as the time that you spend looking for them and dwelling on them. If you're looking for them and focusing on them, they will drive you crazy. If you fixate on those bad habits or unattractive physical and personality qualities, it will be nearly impossible to see anything else.

If you are looking for their positive qualities, you will find those too. Begin a new purpose to notice your spouse's good qualities. Look for the positive character traits in them; they are there too! What you focus on is your choice. You won't regret choosing to focus on the positives. You will be blessed and so will your spouse.

Consider what Paul wrote in Philippians 4:8. *"Finally, brothers, whatever is true, whatever is honorable, whatever is just, whatever is pure, whatever is lovely, whatever is commendable, if there is any excellence, if there is anything worthy of praise, think about these things."*

Imagine if you focused your thoughts on only the good in your spouse. What if you used Philippians 4:8 as a filter through which you looked at your spouse. You could choose to think thoughts that are true, honorable, just, pure, lovely, commendable, excellent, and praiseworthy. Just imagine how beautiful your marriage would be if you thought this way about your spouse. Consider how blessed they would be as you focus on the positive aspects of who they are!

When You See the Good

You will find as much good in your spouse as you seek to find. Seek to view them from God's perspective. When you look for good qualities, they will appear. Don't stop with recognizing these positive attributes. Go a step further and verbalize your positive thoughts. Always be watching for opportunities to uplift your spouse.

Just as no one has your power to destroy your spouse's spirit more than you do, no one has the power to uplift and encourage your spouse more than you do. You know exactly what to say to encourage them. You know exactly how to uplift them and make them feel valued. You have the power to help them believe in themselves and accomplish great things. You can do this with your positive words.

The Apostle Paul challenged the Christians in Ephesus to use their words to build up instead of tear down in Ephesians 4:29: *"Let no corrupting talk come out of your mouths, but only such as is good for building up, as fits the occasion, that it may give grace to those who hear."*

When was the last time you thanked God for your spouse? When was the last time you thanked your spouse for an everyday task they complete? Thankfulness is supposed to be a part of a Christian's life. You will miss many opportunities for thanksgiving in your marriage relationship if you are fixated on your spouse's flaws. Look for opportunities to build up your spouse through thanksgiving.

Here are some areas for which you should be regularly thanking your spouse:
- Going to work
- Cleaning the house
- Providing financially
- Grocery shopping
- Staying within budget
- Giving to you sexually
- Cooking
- Car maintenance
- Setting up doctor's appointments
- Lawn maintenance
- Paying bills
- Working hard
- Disciplining the children
- Washing dishes
- Helping with pets

- Running errands

These are just a few ordinary areas where we often forget to notice the positive aspects of our partner. If we look for good, we will find good. When we see the good, we need to respond in the right way. Yet, often, we neglect to say thank you for the good things they do for us and the hundreds of ways our spouse is there for us. It's all about what you're looking for and what you do when you find it.

Accepting your spouse may seem impossible right now. Begin to make small changes in your focus, thanksgiving, and perception. It becomes much easier to accept your spouse when you are regularly thanking God for them, when you're looking for good, and when you're thanking them for the positives.

God accepts us; we should accept our spouse. It's time to accept them for who they are and who they are not. When you do this, you will begin to create your fairy tale.

9

Who's the Fairest
of Them All?

Me First

Once upon a time . . . a boy and a girl were equally the most selfish of them all.

Thomas

It was year two of our marriage. Lysandra was pregnant with the first of our four beautiful daughters. Since I was a youth pastor of a church that also had a Christian school, we both worked for the church and the school. The staff of the school went together to a teachers' conference in Gatlinburg, Tennessee. I was the only male, driving a fifteen-passenger van full of women, including my pregnant wife, on a trip that turned out to be preparation for my future existence as the only guy in a house full of girls.

123

We pulled into a Golden Corral Buffet late one evening. I was really hungry. I made sure Lysandra and I were first in the door; the smell of the food was calling me. Lysandra and I were also first in line to pay. We finished paying and found a table large enough for our entire group. The other women were in line waiting to pay. They then headed toward the bathroom.

I stood up and told Lysandra, "Let's go, I'm hungry."

Lysandra replied with those wide blue eyes, "I don't think we should go until everyone's here. Let's wait, pray as a group, and then eat together."

I told her, "No, I'm not waiting for who knows how long to eat. It doesn't matter; let's go."

Her concerned eyes pleaded with me as she quietly implored, "Please don't make me go before everyone else. I don't think it's appropriate."

I said, "This is a waste of time. Get up, let's go." She then knew I was serious. She got up and started slowly toward the buffet. When her boss, our school principal, came out from the bathroom and saw her putting food on her plate, she scolded Lysandra and told her how rude she was for not being able to wait a couple of minutes for the rest of the group.

Lysandra took her scolding quietly with a stiff chin, at least in the moment. When we got back to our hotel room that night she was devastated. The emotions she had held in all evening came out like a dam bursting under tremendous pressure. She cried for hours. She was embarrassed, she was hurt, and she was angry.

The fight was on. I was going to win. Remember, I was a winner, and I wasn't afraid to fight dirty back then! I used every angle in the argument from "You are to do what your husband says, not what your boss says" to "I didn't do anything wrong; you're just overreacting because the pregnancy has made you hormonal."

That escalated things very quickly. She cried more, cried harder, and cried louder. I told her to stop crying so loudly; someone would hear her in one of the other rooms. If you've been married for even a few months, you know that telling your wife to stop crying because she's hormonal and embarrassing you doesn't calm her down at all! We went back and forth for a while. Lysandra was clearly looking for an apology from me. I refused. I needed to win, and I truly felt justified. I felt I deserved to eat as soon as I was hungry despite what everyone else was doing. I viewed the entire world with a *me first* mindset.

The truth was, there was no reason for me not to wait a few minutes to eat. I wasn't going to starve to death. I should have listened to my wife begging me to wait, but that would have meant putting her first, and that wasn't how I rolled back then.

I was most certainly in the wrong, but in those early years, you would have never heard me admit that. It was years later when my wife reminded me of this story, which I had completely forgotten about, that I hung my head in shame for my selfishness and finally gave her the long overdue apology that she deserved.

Lysandra

That teachers' conference was undoubtedly a low point in our marriage. There was so much tension. I was constantly concerned about how Thomas was going to act, and he was constantly feeling like he had to fight for himself, because I put everyone else first thanks to my people pleasing lifestyle. We were both so selfish and had no idea, and our selfishness led to a lot of fights!

One of my most *me first* moments in our marriage took place in northern Alabama in July of 2005. Hurricane Dennis was ferociously making its way toward the Alabama coastline. Thomas and I were two Iowa kids living in the South for the first time. We heard on the news to evacuate north so we did. We packed up our Dodge Intrepid, which had a driver's side window stuck in the upright position and no air conditioning.

We were on the interstate along with thousands of other evacuees. Both south bound and north bound sides of the highway were moving north to help get the people out as quickly as possible, and yet we were still in stop-and-go traffic for hours. Keep in mind it was July in Alabama—extremely hot and unbearably humid. We had no AC and Thomas's window was up. He was cranky to say the least.

We finally arrived at a disgusting, cheap motel that we couldn't afford. This shabby motel was in the sketchiest part of Birmingham. It did not feel safe. Neither of us were feeling particularly lovey-dovey. I was sick of being in the car and wanted to go for a walk and do something. I felt like this was the perfect opportunity for a lover's getaway. We might as well make the most of our mandatory evacuation. All Thomas wanted was to lie in the room on the questionable bedspread and watch TV. He was hot and tired, and I was rested and bored.

I begged him to walk with me. We argued, and he won. He wasn't moving. I left the motel room in a huff and went on a walk by myself. I remember feeling uncomfortable and unsafe as I walked around this undesirable neighborhood by myself thinking, "I hope I do get kidnapped and killed; that'll teach him a lesson!"

We were both so selfish. We both had our own agenda as the most important priority. Spoiler, I didn't get kidnapped, so no lesson was learned. We spent two nights in that trashy motel room miserable and silent all because we were both destroying our fairy tale with our prevailing selfishness.

The Revolution of the Earth

You are a selfish being. Your default setting is *me first*. King David reminds us in Psalm 51:4–5, "*Against you, and you only, have I sinned and done what is evil in your sight, so that you may* be justified in your words and blameless in your judgement. Behold, I was brought forth in iniquity, and in sin did my mother conceive me." You were born into sin, falling short of God's standards. That's not an excuse or a get-out-of-jail-free card, but a truth to understand about yourself. You believe the earth revolves around you, and so do I.

If you disagree, take a moment to relive a few of your memories. Your loved one's funeral, for instance. We are certain that as you went to a loved one's funeral you were thinking about how their death affects you, how you looked at the funeral, how others in the family will view your position in life, how tired you are, how long this service might go, how hungry you are, sad you are, or how happy you are now that they're dead. (Hopefully not the last one!)

The only proof you need that the human race is naturally selfish is to consider people's behavior during times of crisis. During the height of corona virus people were buying all the toilet paper they could fit in their cars, with zero thought of anyone else. At the very mention of a hurricane, the store shelves are empty where they used to be filled with bottled water. Not to mention, you haven't drunk a glass of water all year, but now for some reason, you are desperately in need of twenty gallons of it.

The reality of our selfish society is fleshed out every year after the Thanksgiving meal, as people all over this country elbow one another for the last of the discounted televisions.

You are at the center of your world. You are selfish. You put yourself first. We all make ourselves the hero of our own story unless we consciously fight against this natural tendency.

In every situation, no matter how irrelevant you are, you make yourself the main character. You make everything about you. You may not know that you do it. Or maybe you know you make everything about you, and you're quite confident you're right, because everything *is* about you. Either way, you're wrong.

You are not the end-all be-all. Not everything is about you. The earth doesn't revolve around you.

Lysandra

I know it seems ridiculous to be so self-absorbed to make even a loved one's funeral about yourself, and it is, but I'm worse!

Thomas lost his grandma Juanita when I was pregnant with our fourth daughter, Violet. His grandma Juanita was a beautiful lady, inside and out. She was an excellent Grandma to him and all the grandkids. Her loss was felt deeply. To make things more difficult, Thomas had to preach at her funeral while dealing with his own sorrow.

I was so self-centered that I got upset and hurt by him, because he didn't tell me I looked pretty on the day of the funeral. Yeah, I'm that selfish! I was insecure about how I looked that day just like every other day of my life, but it was worse because I was pregnant, hormonal, and nervous to be judged by his whole family. My selfishness was magnified because of a perfect storm of insecurities.

I don't remember saying anything to him about it that day, but I had feelings of hurt and resentment. I took an opportunity to be selfless, show love, and comfort my husband with a pure heart, and I turned it into a pity party for myself.

I was living a *me first* lifestyle. Everything's about me. The earth revolves around me. Me, me, me!

Thomas

I know, by now you're thinking I am a saint for putting up with Lysandra's selfishness for all these years! Don't feel too sorry for me. I was just as selfish or more selfish than she was. We have many stories to prove it.

When we moved back to Iowa after living in Alabama for four years, I was happy to be near my old friends again. Lysandra, myself, our two babies, and one on the way moved into Lysandra's parents' basement in the little town of Walker while we looked for a house to buy in my hometown, Cedar Rapids. We only had one car, so it was challenging trying to accommodate both our schedules during this time.

We left Walker early to go to my parents' house one Saturday morning. We had only been there a short time when my old buddies came over. When they asked me to go hang out with them, I quickly said yes, leaving my pregnant wife at my parents' house with our one-year-old, our baby, and no car. I didn't even think twice. All I knew was that I was excited to spend time with my friends, and it was awesome. It was like just the old days.

We got food, drove around our old neighborhood, and looked around the mall. My friends and I found the funniest shirt. The shirt that would almost cost me my marriage. It was a video game silhouette of a husband and a wife, and it said, "Game Over." I thought it was hilarious. My wife surprisingly enough did not even crack a smile when I showed up hours later wearing the shirt while my buddies all laughed and carried on.

She very seriously said, "It's time to go, NOW!" We said goodbye quickly and got in the car headed back to "Smallville." When the babies were strapped in and the car doors were shut, Lysandra started crying. "How could you?"

"How could I what?"

"How could you abandon me at your mom's house with two small babies and no food or playpen and then tell me that you hate being married to me with that horrible shirt?"

We fought the whole half hour to Walker about the shirt. It ended up in the trash that night.

Looking back now, I can't believe I didn't ask Lysandra if she minded if I left her there with the babies. I didn't ask if she or the kids needed food. I ate out and didn't bring her or the kids anything to eat. I didn't check to see if the girls would need a nap or if they had anything to nap in. I would never do something like that now, but back then I was so selfish.

I thought about one thing that day, how much fun I was going to have.

Self-care in the Extreme

We are all aware of our culture's push toward self-care. You can't watch three commercials without an encouragement to take care of yourself: get that mani/pedi, go to the movies, have a spa day, buy that special something. Tom Haverford summed it up best on *Parks and Recreation* when he said, "Treat yo' self!" We are told by our world to take care of number one, because no one else will. We are constantly bombarded with advertisements to get yourself something nice, buy more, purchase experiences, and think about yourself.

It's not that it's wrong to do something nice for yourself or that it's bad to take care of yourself, but we don't really need the reminder. Our flesh is already wired in a selfish way. A human will always take care of themselves. Paul said this to the Christians in Ephesus in Ephesians 5:29: "*For no one ever hated his own flesh, but nourishes and cherishes it . . .*"

When your subconscious realizes a fight is about to start, it will immediately begin to form arguments, plan an attack, and justify your actions. The heart of you will look out for you! It is your nature. Your default is to defend your stance, actions, opinions, and behavior.

No one needs to tell you to eat when you're hungry, to rest when you're tired, or to have fun when you want to. You naturally think about your own needs and wants. Unless you have a warped view of yourself, you don't need to be reminded to take care of yourself. No one teaches you to fight to have the temperature in the house at a perfectly comfortable setting for yourself.

Vehicle manufacturers understand how selfish we are in our relationships. That's why all current makes and models have separate heating and cooling controls for the driver and the passenger. Most likely this feature has saved many marriages. You will instinctively always make your comfort your number one priority.

You're already constantly thinking of yourself and what you believe is best for you. It is your very nature. You are selfish to the core and it's affecting your relationship.

Here are some simple signs that you're being selfish in your marriage:

- You frequently choose your preference for activities.
- You don't ask your spouse what they think in situations.
- You forget to check on your spouse emotionally for long amounts of time.
- You repeatedly feel your way is best.
- You have little patience with your spouse.
- You have no understanding of your spouse's perspective.
- You don't ask your spouse for their opinion.
- You refuse to admit your own shortcomings.
- You don't take advice from your spouse.
- You'll do whatever it takes to get your way.
- Making your spouse happy is rarely on your mind.
- You rarely say thank you to your spouse.
- It's your way or the highway.
- You become defensive when your choices or opinions are challenged.
- You don't discuss big work or life decisions with your spouse.

Like a Dream

Have you ever woken up from a dream that seems so real and makes perfect sense only to replay that dream and realize it was unrealistic, bizarre, senseless, and even insane? That's what it's like to replay selfish moments years later when you have had time to grow, mature, and reevaluate that same situation.

It's like, "How could I have thought it was okay to react that way? How could I have made that about me when it was clearly about the other person? How could I have been so blindly selfish?" It's almost like waking up from one of those bizarre dreams. It seems to make sense in the moment then you "wake up" and realize your perception of that scenario wasn't reality at all.

You can act like the most selfish person on the planet and believe you are totally justified in your actions. The interesting thing is that when you're in that moment of defending your words, actions, and attitude, you have no idea you're being selfish or have an incorrect perception on the situation. At that moment it all makes so much sense. You have deceived yourself. In his letter, the Apostle John calls us out on it in 1 John 1:8. *"If we say we have no sin, we deceive ourselves, and the truth is not in us."* Don't be deceived by our culture or your own mind; you are a selfish being. You think about yourself first, put your own wants and needs first, and you are constantly seeking to fulfill your own desires.

You naturally have an individual mentality. That doesn't just disappear when you get married. In fact, it is magnified after marriage, because your individual nature is trying to watch out for itself in this new team situation. Jesus's brother James warns us in James 3:14–16 exactly where our selfishness will lead us. *"But if you have bitter jealousy and selfish ambition in your hearts, do not boast and be false to the truth. This is not the wisdom that comes down from above, but is earthly, unspiritual, demonic. For where jealousy and selfish ambition exist, there will be disorder and every vile practice."*

Don't deceive yourself. Recognize your own selfishness, or you will destroy your fairy tale with it.

10

We're in this Castle Together

Keeping a Team Mentality

Once upon a time . . . there were a boy and a girl who became one.

Thomas

#TeamOsterkamp—that's our mantra. We're now a team more than we've ever been before. After years of living a *me first* lifestyle, I reformed. I started intentionally putting Lysandra before myself. It all changed in 2008. We had been married for almost five years and our third daughter Abigail was on the way—she was literally on the way!

We were in the hospital, Lysandra was laboring, the room was quiet and dark as she always preferred it during such intense pain. She had been in labor for twelve hours when the doctor came in to check and see how close the baby was. She demanded an ultrasound machine immediately from the nurse with such a forceful tone that we knew this was incredibly serious.

It was like my entire world stopped even though everything in the room became unbelievably chaotic. Nurses and techs raced into the room; it was full of professionals rushing around following protocol. Meanwhile I was pushed farther and farther away from my wife into the corner of the room.

I could hear my wife shouting frantically, "Is my baby okay? Is my baby okay?"

I was frozen in disbelief and confusion. After two very normal labors and deliveries previously, I fully understood this was really bad. Nothing like this had ever happened before, and I was completely blindsided.

It was in a few short moments that felt like hours when this medical team, with no explanation, rushed my wife out of the room, down the hall, and through a set of double doors that I wasn't welcome to enter. I felt alone in a way I had never felt before. The reality of my helplessness hit me like a speeding bus. Would I ever see my wife alive again? Was my baby going to make it?

I was standing there entirely rigid; I must have looked like a statue. A young nurse broke into my newly upside-down world by saying, "Mr. Osterkamp, Mr. Osterkamp, come with me."

I followed this nurse and listened intently as she filled me in on the situation. My baby had turned breech in the womb during one of the contractions, and my wife was being prepped for an emergency cesarean section. I was now being dressed in a gown, slippers, and hair net, and being led down a hall into the operating room.

I saw her lying there, paralyzed from the neck down. When she looked up at me, I could see the fear in her beautiful blue eyes. I held her limp hand. In that moment, being reunited with the love of my life, it was like everything was different. I had taken her for granted for far too long. I now had a renewed love for Lysandra. In those moments, being faced with the death of my wife, my helpless heart was broken. I would have given my very life to save hers. I saw her as more valuable than myself or anything I wanted. I wanted her!

Because of this emergency life-and-death situation, a transformation took place in my spirit. I now viewed Lysandra as first, and I was second. I would no longer live for me and my way all the time. I would put my wife first. God spared my wife and my daughter. I only regret that it took facing her death to change me. Please don't make the same mistake that I made. Don't wait for that life-and-death moment to truly see how valuable your spouse is.

Now I see Lysandra as first. Now I see our marriage as the true team it was meant to be. Now we're living a realistic fairy tale.

Lysandra

When we came home from the hospital after that surprise c-section, life was different. Not just because of Thomas's revelation, but because the workload in the home had now changed drastically. I was under doctor's orders not to lift, bend, do stairs, or stand for long amounts of time. I was devastated by the news that I could no longer take care of my family or my babies. With a two-year-old, a one-year-old, and an infant at home, there were many needs and chores to be done. The most pressing one of all—laundry.

We had been in the hospital for four days, and with little children you go through laundry at an alarming rate. There were four loads needing to be done when we walked in the door to the house, that beautiful old house. The washer and dryer were located three flights of stairs down in the dungeon of a basement. I couldn't do stairs or carry heavy laundry baskets.

Thomas hadn't done a single load of laundry in the five years we had been married! I had to explain how to treat the stains and use our washer and dryer. He did those four loads of laundry with a happy attitude. I couldn't believe what I was witnessing. He was amazing. He was just so happy the baby and I were healthy.

Thomas had to change all the one-year-old's diapers because I couldn't lift her up or get down on the floor. He had to do dishes, cook, bathe the babies, and everything else you can imagine. The four of us depended on him for everything. A man who enjoyed being served became our servant. The dynamic of our home was turned upside down.

When I asked him to help me or get one of the girls, I was nervous he'd be mad or annoyed, but he was a new Thomas. I could see the love in his eyes. When he looked at me, he was blinking away tears. When he said he loved me, it was different. There was deep passion behind the words and there were actions to back it up.

I felt him putting my needs and well-being first. I became the most important thing in his life—even over himself.

We became a true team, and it was amazing!

Team Mentality

When you walked down the aisle, made your vows, and said *I do*, you ceased to be a one-man show and became a team. Your life is no longer about you and is now about your team. A team isn't about one player. A team is about many talented players working together, considering each other in the game.

Michael Jordan is without a doubt the greatest basketball player to ever live. Even with all his seemingly super-human talent and athletic ability, he was not able to win a championship without the right team. He did not immediately become a champion when he joined the Chicago Bulls in 1984. It was seven long years before he won his first championship. He had such gifted teammates around him, men like Scottie Pippen, Horace Grant, and Dennis Rodman. Only after he learned to trust them was he able to win three championships in a row twice. A player is only as good as the team within which he operates.

You are a fool to devalue your team or your teammate. Your teammate is your most valuable asset. Your team is your strongest advantage. Your spouse is not holding you back from being great; your spouse is what makes you great. Look what King Solomon had to say about this in Proverbs 18:22: *"He who finds a wife finds a good thing and obtains favor from the LORD."* Your spouse is not your enemy, they are a blessing from God.

We're In This Together

The married life is all about the team. Everything we do affects our spouse. If one of you gets a raise, both are blessed by the increase of funds. If one spouse gets fired, both are affected by the lack of income. If one spouse is in pain, both are hindered. If one spouse is in sorrow, both are under a cloud. If one spouse is rejoicing over good news, both are encouraged.

Think of playing a team sport. If one of the teammates is constantly trying to win the spotlight and become the greatest of all, their selfishness will hurt the whole team. They go for the shot to pump up their stats rather than pass the ball to a teammate with a better shot, and it costs them the game. They refuse to work hard on defense because it's not as important to them to help their team as it is to be the one who scores the points.
This me-first, self-centered attitude hurts the team and ultimately hurts them. No one wants to work with them. No one wants to coach them or play alongside them. They are selfish, and everyone near a selfish person gets hurt.

Everything affects everything. Everything you say or don't say affects your spouse. Everything you do or don't do reflects on your spouse. You're now a team and connected on every level.

Are you playing like you even have a teammate? Do you consider how a decision will affect them? Do you think before you say something with the understanding that the words you say will affect your teammate? Are you passing the ball or selfishly taking all the shots you can every time you see an opportunity for yourself?

Put Your Money Where Your Mouth Is

It's not enough to just say we're a team. You must back that up with actions. How do you prove that you're thinking like a team? How do you show that you're putting your spouse first?

Here are some practical ways to show your spouse they are first in your life:
- Put your phone down when they're talking to you.
- Let your spouse set the temperature at home.
- Listen intently to understand, not to reply.
- Ask their opinion.
- Discuss ways to spend free time.
- Ask questions about their feelings.
- Give a tight, non-sexual hug when they've had a rough day.
- Allow your spouse to have control of the remote.
- Don't interrupt them.
- Do it their way.

Lysandra

We often think the way to show our spouse they're first in our lives is in the huge decisions or big gestures. The truth is that proving you have put your spouse first is most meaningful by being consistently selfless in the little everyday, simple ways. If we are acting in humility and putting them first in seemingly simple ways, it will be more natural to act in humility and put them first as a way of life when the big decisions come along.

Thomas and I got on a last-minute flight from Florida to Kansas for a funeral under tragic circumstances. We chose to pack as light as possible carrying only backpacks. When we arrived in Kansas it was after dark and around fifteen degrees. As our hotel was only a mile from the airport, and we were trying to conserve funds, we decided we'd walk rather than spend money on an Uber.

The next morning, we were up early getting ready when I realized I had forgotten to bring a small purse on the trip. I couldn't show up at a somber funeral wearing a teal polka dot backpack. My husband said "I'll go find you a small black purse" before I had even thought of asking.

My loving husband walked a mile to and from Walmart in twenty-degree weather wearing only a light jacket to purchase a small black purse for me. I remember getting ready in the hotel thinking, "I can't believe how amazing Thomas is now! He loves me so much and would do anything for me. I'm so blessed!"

It is these simple everyday ways that my husband shows me that I am first. These mundane acts of kindness produce colossal trust and confidence in the love of my husband.

Thomas is an amazing husband. I no longer worry and fret about whether or not he'll consider me in his decisions or anything else in life. He puts me first consistently. He thinks of me and asks my opinions. He takes my advice. He cares about my needs and my wants as well.

Thomas

Lysandra is the most selfless person I know. She will dish out all the food to the rest of us and eat nothing if it appears there won't be enough food to go around. She will stay up late preparing birthday parties and Christmas festivities to make them spectacular for the rest of us.

I love Iowa Hawkeye football! One of my favorite places to be on a fall day is inside of Kinnick Stadium with seventy thousand of my closest friends. Even though it's not something that Lysandra enjoys, she would get me tickets to a game almost every year that we lived in Iowa. And she didn't just get me tickets, she dressed up in Hawkeye gear from head to toe and came to the game with me.

While at the game, she didn't sit there and look miserable, even though she was probably dying on the inside. She screamed and cheered, not always for the right team, but she was trying. She put her whole heart into it because she knew that it was something that I really loved to do.

I never wonder if Lysandra will put my needs above her own. That's just how she lives her life. She makes my phone calls, takes care of all my stuff, she orders the food at the drive thru so that I don't have to talk to people, creates a peaceful home for me and the girls, she completely spoils me, and takes care of everything I could ever need.

Think Like a Team

Acting like a team begins with thinking like a team. Thinking like a team doesn't happen naturally. You lived your entire life up until marriage thinking about life from the perspective of one, only to be thrown into this new team. The way you think must change.

You no longer should have thoughts like, "What do I want to do?" "How will this affect me?" or "Will this benefit me?" The new thought process should sound like this, "What will my spouse want to do?" "How will this affect my spouse?" and "Will this benefit us as a team?"

Our thoughts should no longer be natural and me-centered but divine like Christ's. We see this clearly in Philippians

2:1-8:

> *So if there is any encouragement in Christ, any comfort from love, any participation in the Spirit, any affection and sympathy, complete my joy by being of the same mind, having the same love, being in full accord and of one mind. Do nothing from selfish ambition or conceit, but in humility count others more significant than yourselves. Let each of you look not only to his own interests, but also to the interests of others. Have this mind among yourselves, which is yours in Christ Jesus, who, though he was in the form of God, did not count equality with God a thing to be grasped, but emptied himself, by taking the form of a servant, being born in the likeness of men. And being found in human form, he humbled himself by becoming obedient to the point of death, even death on a cross.*

We will be blessed when we think like Jesus. When thinking like Jesus, we will no longer be motivated by selfish ambition or conceit but by humility. Jesus's thoughts are toward our interests. That's why He died on a cross. He was thinking of you when He submitted Himself to such pain and suffering and eventual death. There is no greater act of humility than giving your very life for someone. This is the way we are instructed to think about our spouse.

Putting your spouse first sounds great. We can all agree that it's the right thing to do. However, when the time comes to actually put them first, it can feel less important than what we want in that moment.

Think about the temperature at which you set your house. Do you talk about it? Do you compromise? Is one spouse constantly bundled up and uncomfortable? Is one spouse hot, sweaty, and miserable? Can you change your mindset to be more sacrificial like Christ and take the hit so your spouse will be comfortable? The literal temperature of the house can set the figurative temperature of the home.

Consider what you watch on television or movie night. Is there one spouse who automatically gets power of the remote control? Are you always watching a certain spouse's favorite genre while the other sits quietly disappointed? It's time to change your thinking to be humble like Jesus and pass that remote off to your spouse.

Let's talk about sex. There is no greater opportunity to be selfish in marriage than in the bedroom. Is one spouse frequently enjoying sex more than the other? Are both partners finding satisfaction when you have sex? Is one spouse making all the decisions about what your sexual relationship looks like? Is one partner seeking their own pleasure rather than the pleasure of their spouse and the gratification of the team? The time has come for you to think like Jesus even in the bedroom. It's time to put your spouse's needs above your own when you participate in intimacy.

Examine time management in your relationship. Is your time being assigned and proportioned to your priorities with little or no thought to your spouse or the team? Who creates the time budget in your home? Is there discussion, communication, and compromise with regards to how you spend your time? Maybe you need to rethink your time management in the mind of Christ and create a new time budget with your spouse's best interests at heart.

When attempting to put your spouse first as Jesus put us first, the most difficult areas are the little routine ones. If faced with a gun pointed at your spouse, you probably wouldn't hesitate in your mind to take the bullet for your love. But watching an action/adventure rather than a romantic comedy is too great a sacrifice.

It feels like there would be zero consideration about whether or not to jump in front of a car to save your spouse's life;

you would take that hit without question. But giving your spouse the time and touch they need to feel satisfied when having sex is an unreasonable expectation for you to fulfill.

The mindset of Jesus was not only sacrificial in His major, most significant act of love, taking our sin and dying on that cross. Jesus's mindset was also consistently sacrificial in the way He lived in the everyday, mundane moments. He stopped and took time to talk to the broken, He listened to the blind, He had compassion on the hurting. He forfeited satisfying His hunger for food to show His love to the crowds of needy people. Jesus sacrificed the comfort of a home and bed to serve the ones He loved. He lived his life consistently sacrificial moment by moment. This is living with the mind of Christ.

If you want to create your fairy tale rather than destroy it, you must stop thinking *me first* and start thinking like Christ— *others first.*"

Conclusion

Happily Ever After

Once upon a time . . . there were a boy and girl who got married and lived happily ever after.

Your Happily Ever After Starts Now

You can begin creating your happily ever after today. It's not too late for you! Your marriage relationship may be broken and seem irreparable. It may feel like it's too late for redemption. You may believe it's impossible to enjoy a happily ever after. Jesus reminds us in Luke 18:27, *"What is impossible with man is possible with God."* He is the God of the impossible.

Don't believe the lie that your marriage is too broken to be repaired. Don't buy into the lie that marriage can't be awesome. Have faith in the God of the impossible. Jesus said in Luke 1:37, *"For nothing will be impossible with God."* He wants to create a fairy tale in your marriage. Trust Him and give Him the permission and freedom to work in your relationship. Invite Him in.

As you allow God to move in your relationship and to change you, evaluate yourself. Are you destroying the fairy tale God wants to create?

What Are You Seeking?

Take a moment to examine your definition of a fairy tale. If your definition is seeking your own happiness forever, you are destroying your fairy tale. Seeking your own happiness will bring only sadness and sorrow. A life lived for oneself is a miserable life.

Imagine if you and your spouse seek God first in every aspect of your life. Think how that would change the direction of your marriage. When you both seek God, you are walking a path, heading in the same direction, becoming closer to God and therefore closer to each other. You are in harmony with God and therefore in harmony with one another. Imagine how peaceful your marriage could be.

Change your definition of your fairy tale today. Make God's plan your purpose. Leave your chase for happiness in the dust and chase after God today. Start anew today and permit God to create a true fairy tale.

What Do You Expect?

Sit in silence for a brief time and allow your mind to discover the expectations hidden in your heart. You have known and unknown expectations. Evaluate the known and uncover the unknown. Ask yourself if your expectations are reasonable or unreasonable.

You were disenchanted after the honeymoon was over. Marriage wasn't everything you thought it would be. Grieve the loss of unmet expectations. Let go of unreasonable expectations. Take your sorrow to God and leave it there. Ask Him to heal your broken heart.

Set your spouse free from your expectations today. Release your unreasonable expectations. Be happy in Jesus. Find true joy and inner peace from your relationship with Him. It's okay if your spouse makes you happy, but don't rely on them for your happiness. It's not too late to apologize for expecting too much of your spouse.

Imagine how liberating it will be for both of you to drop expectations. Think about the relief of no longer living a life of disappointment. Imagine how beautiful contentment in your relationship will feel. Consider how your spouse will feel when you free them from your expectations. Your fairy tale will be created.

How Many Dragons Must You Slay?

Evaluate your style of fighting. If you are a competitive person, you may feel the need to fight every battle and win. If you are a peacekeeper, you may feel the need to lie about your feelings so no one gets upset. Neither of these are healthy ways to view conflict.

Fighting should be present in marriage, but all fighting should be over only worthwhile issues and to accomplish resolution, not to win. You don't need to slay every dragon. Choose your battles carefully. Think about the way you fight, disagree, argue, or discuss things. Are you fighting fair in appropriate ways and at appropriate times? If not, have a calm discussion about the way you fight. Apologize for your own inappropriate fighting habits. Share the ways you want to change how you fight.

Imagine if you each stopped fighting every battle. Consider the impact on your home if you started fighting fairly. Think of the peace that could be present if you fought for resolution. Imagine the lovely fairy tale you could create out of that new peaceful environment.

Did You Marry a Frog or a Prince?

The truth is you didn't marry a frog or a prince/princess. You married a person who sometimes acts like a frog and sometimes acts like a prince/princess. Your spouse has areas to grow in just as you do. Be honest with yourself, are you trying to change your spouse?

It's time to stop trying to change your spouse and accept them for who they are and who they are not. God didn't make a mistake when He created your spouse. Accept His design. Love your spouse the way Jesus loves you.

Imagine the relief of not working constantly to change your spouse. Think about the relaxing life you could enjoy by simply being grateful to God for your spouse. Consider how your spouse would feel if you began to thank them rather than pick them apart. Pray right now a prayer of acceptance for the partner God gave you, then watch your fairy tale begin to form.

Who's First Around Here?

Reflect on your selfishness. We are all self-centered people. Some of us fight our selfish tendencies more than others. Examine your behavior. How selfish are you? Maybe as you look over the past few years, you realize you have been thinking of yourself first in most situations. Maybe you've been acting like you're the only one on the team.

We must all seek to think like Jesus—sacrificial and humble. It's time to put your spouse first. You can change to a team mentality today. Allow your spouse to make a decision, set the temperature, or choose where you go. Think of their needs before your own.

Imagine if you started acting like the team you were created to be! Think of how well your marriage would function if you two acted as one flesh like the Creator designed you to be. Consider how your spouse would feel if you began to put their needs before your own consistently in everyday, routine ways. You may find yourself living in a real-life fairy tale.

Happily Ever After

Happily ever after is achieved when happiness is not pursued. Happily ever after is achieved when we seek God above all else. It is grasped when we release unreasonable expectations. It becomes a reality when we fight only worthwhile fights, not for victory but for resolution. It can be enjoyed when we stop trying to change our spouse and accept them for who they are. Happily ever after is achieved when we think like Jesus and put ourselves last while selflessly putting our spouse first. This is how to create a fairy tale that ends with "and they lived happily ever after."

About Family Meeting

Our desire is to help you have the meaningful relationships that you desire in your marriage and family.

Thomas Osterkamp, Lead Pastor at Beachside Community Church in Palm Coast, FL is married to his childhood sweetheart Lysandra. They have been serving God in pastoral ministry for several years.

Lysandra and Thomas have four beautiful, spunky, funny girls: Kathryne, Isabella, Abigail, and Violet. Their house is always busy, dramatic, exciting, and full of love.

The Family Meeting Podcast is a podcast all about family relationships. Thomas and Lysandra invite you to be a part of their family. They pull back the curtain on their family life to share practical tips and advice on everything from marriage, parenting, sex, and everything in between. For helpful posts, videos, podcast show notes, or to book them to speak at your next event, go to www.familymeeting.org.

End Notes

1. Susanna Newsonen, Why the Happiness Chase is Making You Unhappy: Three Ways to Stop the Chase and Start the Fulfillment (Psychology Today psychologytoday.com, 2017)

2. Dr. Tony Evans, Kingdom Marriage: Connecting God's Purpose with Your Pleasure (Carol Stream, Illinois: Tyndale House Publishers, 2016), 4-5.

3. Francis and Lisa Chan, You and Me Forever: Marriage in Light of Eternity, (United States: Claire Love Publishing, 2014), 11.

4. Chan, You and Me Forever, 22.

5. June Hunt, Marriage: To Have and to Hold (Peobody, Massachusetts: Hendrickson Publishers, 2014), 39.

6. Penn and Kim Holderness, Everybody Fights: So Why Not Get Better at It? (United States: Thomas Nelson, 2021), 68.

7. Hunt, Marriage, 41.

8. Craig and Amy Groeschel, From This Day Forward: Five Commitments to Fail-Proof Your Marriage, (Grand Rapids, Michigan: Zondervan, 2014), 53.

9. Martha Peace, The Excellent Wife: A Biblical Perspective, (Bemidji, Minnesota: Focus Publishing Inc, 1999), 24.

10. Peace, The Excellent Wife, 24.

11. Peace, The Excellent Wife, 26.

Made in the USA
Columbia, SC
02 August 2023

21093954R00085